Three Million More?

Three Million More?

GUNTHER LAWRENCE

1970

Doubleday & Company, Inc.

GARDEN CITY, NEW YORK

Library of Congress Catalog Card Number 68–22533
Copyright © 1970 by Gunther Lawrence
All Rights Reserved
Printed in the United States of America
First Edition

To my wife Leah

Preface

The tale of American involvement in the dilemma of the Russian Jew may be characterized as one of watchful concern.

President John F. Kennedy, however, offered the brightest hope in recent annals because of his familiarity with the problem and his willingness to offer assistance, an episode that will be discussed between these covers. Three days before his tragic death, Jewish leaders met in Washington to plan a united protest on behalf of Soviet Jews, confident that with such a popular figure as the President to serve as a rallying point, the Kremlin could be persuaded to ameliorate its various discriminations against Jews.

With the sympathetic, but politically alert President Lyndon B. Johnson, the inescapable philosophy of practical politics was exemplified in his statement to the heads of collective Jewish organizations: "There is nothing easier to do than speak. All you have to do is open your lips. But to speak wisely and effectively, that's different."[1]

President Nixon's contribution to this forum of opinion was a campaign statement in 1968, when he told the presidents of twenty-two national Jewish organizations that diplomatic channels could be employed to convey American concern over the plight of Russia's three million Jews. The only American President to have directly pleaded the cause of Soviet Jews was Dwight D. Eisenhower at his meeting with Nikita Khrushchev on September 25, 1959, at Camp David. Eisenhower told the Premier that Jewish groups had expressed deep concern to him regarding the status of Soviet Jews. Khrushchev dismissed the matter by saying that Jews in his country were treated as everyone else was. In a similar conversation, Secretary of State Christian Herter received the standard Kremlin reply from Andrei Gromyko: "It's an internal matter."

Yet nations can be moved. Even the U.S.S.R., with the stereotyped response of "It's an internal matter," is sensitive to international public opinion, especially today, in its desire for increased trade and a *détente* with the West. Prime Minister Harold Wilson, of Great Britain, discovered this to be true during a Moscow visit in June 1963. Wilson, at that time the head of the Labour Party, accused the Russians and Khrushchev of being "barbarians" for keeping families who had been separated during World War II, divided. The protest resulted in several individuals receiving emigration visas to be united with loved ones in England.

A more dramatic response was represented by the late West German Chancellor, Konrad Adenauer, who visited Moscow in 1954. *"Der Alte"* refused to discuss the establishment of diplomatic relations until Soviet leaders agreed to repatriate Russians of German origin still living in special settlements and forced-labor camps. On

August 29, 1954, the Soviet presidium ordered full re-habilitation of nearly two million German nationals. Jews in the Soviet Union, however, are "punished" both as a religious group and as a nationality. Under the former, they are restricted by harsh, anti-religious laws, suffering far more than members of the Eastern Orthodox Church, Baptists, Muslims and others. As a nationality, they receive few cultural benefits, lack schools of their own and are discriminated against in employment and secondary education.

Within the Soviet system even liberally oriented in-tellectuals admit an anti-Semitic holdover from Tsarist days within the Kremlin leadership. In a recent, privately circulated essay, one of the U.S.S.R.'s distinguished phys-icists, Andrei D. Sakharov, called the "backsliding into anti-Semitism" disgraceful, and conceded that in the elite of the Russian Government the spirit of anti-Semi-tism had never fully been dispelled after the 1930s.[2]

Another voice, Yevgeny Yevtushenko, in his celebrated poem, *Babi Yar*, calls attention to the mass murder of thousands of Russian Jews in an unmarked ravine on the outskirts of Kiev. His plea stirred Soviet intellec-tuals and youth, and brought him into disfavor with Khrushchev. In one of several encounters with the Krem-lin leader, Yevtushenko implored: "We cannot go forward to Communism with such a heavy load as Judeophobia, and here there can be neither silence nor denial." The poet told Khrushchev that he personally witnessed acts of anti-Semitism in the U.S.S.R.[3]

In presenting the case for Soviet Jewry, one encounters historical, political, religious and cultural factors that make comprehension difficult for the layman. Then, there is the ever-present apathy. No mass physical violence exists in the Soviet Union's campaign that would cause it to be equated with the Nazis. Testifying before the Foreign Affairs Committee of the House of Representatives, May 10, 1965, Rabbi Joachim Prinz, then chairman of the Conference of Presidents of Major American Jewish Organizations said,

"Only in one sense—in terms of ultimate purpose—may it be said that the policies of Hitlerism and of the Soviet Government are alike: both have sought the elimination of the Jewish presence in history; both have sought in our lifetimes to bring to a close the long Jewish religious and cultural expression."[4]

Upon arriving in the Soviet Union, following a visit to Auschwitz, I had to agree with a parallel drawn by Rabbi Jacob K. Shankman, president of the World Union for Progressive Judaism, who said, after his own encounter with Russian Jews: "One was genocide of the flesh, and the other is genocide of the spirit."[5]

In August 1966, in the company of twenty-two Reform rabbis of the Central Conference of American Rabbis, we returned home after a five-week tour of the Soviet Union and Eastern Europe, where we had hoped to explore the status and condition of the Jew. As with many before us, we had been disturbed by the wide range of charges centered on the U.S.S.R.'s religious and cultural discrimination against a population of more than three million Jews.

The problem dismayed figures from all walks of life, and as for Jews elsewhere, not since the Nazi holocaust and the emergence of the state of Israel, had they been so united as over the plight of their brethren in the U.S.S.R.

They knew that the threat challenged the survival of Jews everywhere. Particularly sensitive were the United States' five and a half million Jews, still conscience-stricken over their apathy during the early days of the Hitler era.

The Jewish protest has spread throughout the world and found adherents among capitalists and Communists, Jews and Christians, statesmen and scholars. A dispatch in the New York *Times* reported on August 1, 1965, nearly a year after the organized and widely publicized American Jewish protest movement, that the Soviet Union was clearly on the defensive about its Jewish population. *Times* correspondent Peter Grose said foreign pressure could receive much of the credit.

The campaign has produced some token concessions: cessation of the economic trials; a few, annually produced books in Yiddish; some emigration; a greater availability of matzos (unleavened bread) for the observance of Passover; and the recent visit to the United States of Moscow's Chief Rabbi, Yehuda Leib Levine.

Despite an effective grass-roots program of education, the *ad hoc* Jewish effort, under the banner of the American Jewish Conference on Soviet Jewry, still leaves unanswered questions. Too many people view the problem from the vantage point of a Western mind, unmindful of the Communist system and the background and history of the problem.

A typical Western Jew might ask, "Why protest for the

return of Yiddish culture when we ourselves have abandoned it?" Some say, "Isn't the Russian campaign really a part of Communism's drive toward atheism and the determination to eliminate all religions?" The liberal Jew wonders why he should protest so loudly for stagnant Orthodoxy. "After all," he says, "we have deserted the ritualistic dogmas of our forefathers in order to harmonize our Jewish faith with modern times. How can any youngster be attracted to this old-fashioned Orthodoxy which I have rejected?" Some contend that the Russian Jew is caught up in the general Communist process of assimilation, an argument advanced by the Soviets.

Thus, the need seemed obvious for a lay approach to, and a consolidation of, an exceedingly difficult subject. Most people are aware that a problem of some sort exists. To understand it, one needs the complete picture in perspective. It is the author's hope that this is contained in the pages that follow.

ACKNOWLEDGMENTS

To bring a work of this sort "to book," as it were, the assistance and good will of many people were required. To mention them all would be, in some cases, to violate pledges of privacy and security.

They know who they are—the ones who found freedom in the West, those who did not—and they will know how deep lies the author's appreciation.

Of incalculable value was the editorial guidance and counsel of Joseph Gale, a critic and bureau chief of the *Evening News*, Newark, New Jersey, to whom I am profoundly grateful.

Particular thanks are due to Dr. Moshe Decter, and to Mr. Emanuel Litvinoff and his quarterly journal, *Jews in Eastern Europe*, both gifted authorities in this field. Also appreciation to Rabbi Robert Seltzer for verifying the historical narrative and to Rabbi George B. Lieberman for his wisdom and counsel.

Vitally concerned and most co-operative were the American Jewish Conference on Soviet Jewry, The American Jewish Committee, The American Jewish Congress and B'nai B'rith and their professional personnel, Philip Baum, Abe Bayer, Jerry Goodman, Philip Katz, Dr. William Korey, Bernard Simon and Morton Yarmon. A special word of thanks to Isaiah M. Minkoff, executive vice-chairman of the National Jewish Community Relations Advisory Council.

I also wish to acknowledge with gratitude the valuable research departments of various universities in Israel and such researchers, translators, editorial and secretarial assistants as: Mrs. Zeke Segal, Mrs. Richard G. Hirsch, Mrs. Greta Fleming, Miss Elaine Rehaut and Mrs. Sanford Zwickler.

Finally, a special word of appreciation to the Central Conference of American Rabbis and to Rabbis Jacob Weinstein and Sidney Regner, and forty-one other companions who helped make a trip to the Soviet Union the memorable event it was, deepening my own sensitivity and concern for my more than three million fellow Jews sealed in the Soviet Union.

Contents

The Uzbek Outrages. Religious Targets. Attacks on the Bible and Rituals. Closing of Synagogues. Restrictions on Passover Matzos. The Innocent Messengers. The Russian Orthodox Church. The Status of Other Religions.

The Dangerous Identity Card. The Cultural Desert. Sovietish Heimland. Reactions from the West. Sholom Aleichem. The Need for Cultural Restoration. The Germans in Russia. The Lack of Educational Facilities. Soviet Response; Jewish Rebuttal. A Teacher's Story.

The Thirty-million Ruble Robbery. Other "Criminal" Cases. The Concern of the Late Bertrand Russell. "No Mercy for Thieves."

Intensification of Anti-Semitism. The Ancient "Enemy"—Zionism. The UN and the Creation of Israel. Turn-About-Face. The Split. The Hope That Is Israel.

Other Anti-Semitic Literature.

The Meeting with Dobrynin. The Presidents' Conference.

Three Million More?

I
American Visitors

"How dare they steam open our mail?" the woman fumed, enjoying her new-found, but short-lived intellectual freedom in Czechoslovakia. She described her experiences for a radio audience. "It's worthy of the old days!" she said. The program moderator called an unlisted number to query whether a government censor office really existed. The man who answered vehemently denied any such thing. A few minutes later, the comrade supervisor of the non-existent mail project telephoned and berated the moderator for misleading his listeners. He then proceeded to describe his mail-peeping service to the radio audience in great detail.[1]

Travelers behind the Iron Curtain seldom take the existence of police-state techniques seriously. They do exist, although they are often difficult to detect.

During the early days of open tourism in the Soviet Union, suspicious persons were undoubtedly kept under surveillance. The procedure is not so simple now as Western tourists stream into Eastern nations for vacations, cultural exchanges or professional visits. All Soviet tourism is handled by the state agency, which appears to have two important functions, that of keeping the foreigner so busy touring, eating and viewing entertainment that he has no time for anything else, and of creating a friendly, deceptively innocent isolation. This does not mean you are not permitted to roam about on your own. Your are. Not many foreigners are that adventurous, however. Furthermore, the language barrier and foreign-news-media isolation make one completely dependent upon his Intourist guide or upon members of his own party. Secondly, whenever you make a request not in your original itinerary, you find it almost impossible to budge the Russian bureaucracy.

It does not take long for a newcomer to become indoctrinated into the Soviet system of regimentation. As we arrived at Sheremetyevo, Moscow's international airport, the customs official immediately handed us forms on which we were told to list every item of currency and jewelry in our possession. One member of the group had a difficult time convincing the systematic Russian mind that, yes, she carried two watches, but one was worn on her dress and was, therefore, ornamental. The official could not comprehend why anyone would use a timepiece for any but a functional purpose. After a lengthy discussion, he shrugged his shoulders and let it go as a capitalistic idiosyncracy.

The Russian Psyche

Understanding their psyche is an essential part of dealing with Russians, especially in any official capacity. Another member of our party, Rabbi George B. Lieberman, of Rockville Centre, New York, returning to his native land for the second time in a decade, said, "According to our standards, honesty is exalted. In their society it is not even expected." As an illustration, he cited the difference between an American and Russian plane traveler. "In the United States," he said, "you sit next to a perfect stranger, and after general comments about the weather and take-off, you engage in a friendly conversation. By the time you land, you have gained an X-ray view of your neighbor. You learned his occupation, the number of bathrooms in his house, the stocks he invests in and even about his mother-in-law. A Russian traveler would be reluctant to engage in conversation. In the Soviet Union, intimacies are seldom shared, even among the best of friends. On the contrary, when a Russian speaks to a visitor, frequently he will lie. He knows that you are aware he is lying, but he is so glib and smooth that for him the falsehoods involve no problem of ethics or morality. This is part of the Russian psyche."

We met our Intourist guide, a short, stocky, round-faced man, outside the customs barrier. "I will be your guide during your visit in the Soviet Union. My name is Sergei," he said. We soon learned to call him "Is Possible Sergei," since this was his reply to most requests. At the appropriate time, his stock answer would be: "Is not possible." His frayed suit, the only one he wore during our fourteen-day trip, became a familiar sight. His authoritarian manner made some of us think he might be a member of KGB (the Soviet secret police), particularly when he would disappear the day before our departure for a new city, ostensibly to pave the way for us.

Sergei showed us another Russia character trait—dual definitions between East and West. During one bus trip, Rabbi W. Gunther Plaut, of Toronto, asked why there were no telephone books in Soviet hotel rooms or other public places. He snapped back: "We don't have telephone books, because in the Soviet Union we believe in freedom, and by not having your number available you're assured of privacy, and this means freedom." Once, during dinner, a member of our party, unable for health reasons to eat the dark Russian bread, tried in vain to exchange the pumpernickel for white bread. Finally, Rabbi Jacob Weinstein of San Francisco, then President of The Central Conference of American Rabbis, walked into the kitchen, and in his limited Russian, tried his luck with three food checkers. No one dared exchange one slice of bread for another until he had the approval of his superiors.

A "Very Special-Interest Group"

The average tourist would never experience the rigid scrutiny, tight scheduling and emotional encounters to which we were exposed. "We were a special-interest group," Rabbi Weinstein said, "concerned with the status of our coreligionists."

The Russians were prepared for our visit. In typical Western fashion we had written scores of letters to Soviet officials informing them of our arrival and seeking appointments. We did not know about the Russian custom of ignoring most communications unless permission to answer them had been received through channels.

Three of us even visited the Soviet embassy in Washington to explain the particular credentials of our group. Rabbi Eugene Mihaly of the Hebrew Union College—Jewish Institute of Religion, defined the broader interests of a modern clergyman, which extend into such areas as world peace, civil rights, urban renewal and mental health. In our discussions we learned of the Russian familiarity with the CCAR pronouncements, particularly the Reform rabbis' championing of the Negro cause and the outspoken criticism of American policy in Vietnam. We sought assistance in trying to arrange appointments with members of the U.S.S.R. intelligentsia, such as Yevsei Liberman (the economist), novelist Illya Ehrenburg (since deceased) and the poet, Yevgeny Yevtushenko.

After listening politely for more than an hour, the suave Anatole Mishkov, the first secretary, suggested we make all arrangements through Intourist, where we were told little could be done, since Intourist's only function was tourism. Perhaps naïvely, we prepared an itinerary of places we wished to visit and people we desired to see, submitting this at the suggestion of Intourist for reference to Moscow. When we arrived, Sergei quickly told us that on the following morning an appointment had been arranged for a delegation of our members to meet with an official of the Ministry of Cults to review the appointments we had requested. Although politely received, the Rabbis discovered they could not penetrate the categorical Russian mind. Once you are classified as a clergyman, your only contact should be with places and individuals relating to religion.

We were told that appointments with intellectuals
would be difficult to arrange because of the summer
vacation schedule, but Sergei kept us dangling until the
last day of our visit with the possibility that such meetings might be arranged. The delegation was told Yevtushenko was out of the city. Yet, on the following morning
we learned from a friend traveling with a large "People
to People" exchange group that they had been introduced
to the poet at a special reception the night before.

Surveillance

Is the tourist really followed and watched? On our
second night in Moscow we decided to worship at two
small suburban congregations. Only four members in
our party agreed to visit the large Central Synagogue to
inform Rabbi Yehuda Leib Levin of our arrival. Our bus
and Intourist guide had been dismissed. Sergei knew
where we intended to go for the evening. He assisted us
in writing out the addresses of the synagogues, so that
taxicab drivers would have no difficulty in understanding
us.

Although it is permissible for a Reform Jew to travel
on the Sabbath, we always made certain not to arrive
at a place of worship in any vehicle in order not to
offend Orthodox Jews of the local congregations. None
of the cabs seemed to know the whereabouts of the
suburban synagogues. They traversed the city blocks as
if they were lost until the members of our party, in
frustration, mentioned the name and address of the
Central Synagogue. Suddenly our taxi driver regained

his sense of direction and immediately headed for the house of worship. As we walked up the steps, we could see we had been expected since a delegation of Russian Jews was waiting to greet us.

Frequently, the Intourist guides could not watch us so closely (or, at least, so we thought). Several mornings, instead of forty-three persons showing up for the morning tour, a handful would be missing. When Sergei asked where everybody was, we would merely report the illness of some in our party. Actually, these individuals had hurried off to special appointments at addresses of people obtained from friends in the United States. Suspicious that they might be followed, one couple changed taxicabs three times. I remember going with Rabbi Lieberman and my wife on such a trip. We called on an old woman, a relative of a friend back home. Her neighbor was visiting, too. Rabbi Lieberman suggested that he engage the neighbor in conversation as a precaution against the neighbor being an informer while we took our hostess aside to present her with a gift.

Informers

The Soviet system of watching guests, or keeping a protective cordon around local citizens, has been carefully planned to avoid detection. After numerous discussions with citizens in Russia and other Eastern European countries one begins to piece together the police methods used so effectively. All tourist hotels are staffed with informers, most of whom are clerks, porters and chambermaids. They have been forced into service as part of reduced or suspended sentences. Some are government officials out of favor who, through such service, expect to be restored to confidence. They are given a simple assignment: to observe foreign visitors and report any suspicious action. To discourage anything but designated contacts with a foreigner, authorities, on the excuse that "We must protect our guests," demand that a resident visiting a stranger surrender his identity card to the clerk until he leaves.

Upon arrival at his hotel the tourist fills out an immigration form and presents his passport to the clerk. The passport will be returned twenty-four hours later—after the clerk has sent it to the Foreign Ministry where the name is checked against a list of "interesting strangers" collected by members of the diplomatic corps throughout the world and by "friends" in foreign countries. If a visitor's name is on such a list, his telephone will be tapped, he will be followed, his visitors checked and his rooms searched.

The same espionage complex applies to citizens in the U.S.S.R. and Eastern European nations. A neighbor, a janitor or a co-worker will function in the same watchdog capacity. After a stranger or foreigner is received in a home, the Russian's next-door neighbor will engage him in innocent conversation and then report the discussion to a superior stationed nearby. A few days later the authorities pay the citizen a visit and pose specific questions about his guest. If the story does not check with that of the informant, appropriate action is taken. In any event, the visit is recorded.

For example, a university professor from Kiev walked

with me in the park and told me how an old friend would repeatedly engage him in conversation, especially after a trip abroad. One day the companion pressed him to relate his political opinions. The professor became suspicious and inquired, "Why do you ask me so many questions? It seems more like an interrogation than a friendly conversation." His friend suddenly broke down and cried: "They asked me to inform on you. I was forced into it in order to reduce my brother's sentence. But believe me, I only gave good reports about you."

"The Invisible Millions"

It is difficult, therefore, to communicate adequately and to obtain information from Russian Jews. Those in the synagogue are harassed elderly pensioners, carefully watched by informers. The only other openly Jewish address is the office of *Sovietish Heimland,* the monthly Yiddish magazine. There, members of the editorial staff are all avowed atheists and trusted Soviet citizens. To reach the remaining Jewish group, which we called "the invisible millions," one must seek them out at Yiddish vaudeville concerts or carry some means of Jewish identification—a yarmulka (skull cap), a Yiddish newspaper under the arm or an El Al flight bag. Only twice a year do thousands of young Jews turn up at the Moscow synagogue, during High Holy Day services and at the festival of Simchas Torah (Rejoicing over the Torah), observed as part of the Festival of Sukkos. Some Jews, if they know who you are, might seek you out. Except for the young Jew bubbling with optimism and unmindful of the lingering past, most are fearful and cautious about communicating with strangers until they are absolutely certain of his loyalty. Natanovich Andreevich, imprisoned during the Stalin era, reminds us, "There is hardly a Jew in the U.S.S.R. who would put his fate at stake by complaining to a foreigner about anti-Semitism or such allied matters." Andreevich, now living in Great Britain, was arrested in 1947 and sentenced to seven years after a school friend informed on him. He was released after Stalin's death. Andreevich points out that even after the fall of the Khrushchev government in 1964, many Jews who remained imprisoned for similar offenses were not released. He stressed that this condition, of which Russian Jews are fully aware, makes them even less talkative. "Fear lingers everywhere. It is so strong that a Jew will share his innermost thoughts only when he is alone with you, face to face."[2]

A member of our group made careful preparations to see an old friend, a writer. They met on the outskirts of Moscow and drove about in the friend's car to make certain they would not be overheard. As a precaution, when they drove off, the Russian Jew looked under the hood of his car to make sure no bugging device had been installed. Each time they stopped for a traffic light and another car pulled alongside, the friend would stop taking or make innocent small talk. He told the American how the Jewish community yearned for information about Israel and Jews elsewhere. (Lately, they have been able to gather information from tourists and the overseas broadcasts of the Voice of America, BBC and Kol Yisrael.) He told the visitor how, in the presence of fellow writers, he would not partake of vodka for fear that his tongue might loosen and he might say something which could be misinterpreted and used against him. He applies the rule even to his own family, saying, "I don't imagine my son or wife would ever inform on me, but they (the government) still have ways."

Hidden Fear

Until one encounters such fear it is difficult to believe that it exists. We met a young Jewish woman wearing an Israeli flag pinned to her jacket. We embraced her. She was pleased to meet not only foreigners who could provide her with interesting news, but surprised to see young, attractive and beardless rabbis so unlike the sterotype with which she was familiar. Anxious to extend her friendship, the young lady invited a number of the rabbis to her home. A member of our party asked her, "Aren't you afraid to bring foreigners into your home?" In her naïveté she replied, "Why should I be?"

The rabbis had a delightful evening. They provided their hostess with a broad description of life in America, including the viable Jewish community. One rabbi noticed that the woman had a small record collection and seemed particularly interested in American jazz (favorite of many young people in the U.S.S.R.). He asked for her name and address so that when he returned to the States he could send her some records. As they departed, she promised to visit the next day at the hotel to say good-by, but when she came into the lobby her smile had disappeared. She ran up to one of the rabbis pleading for the return of the scrap of paper with her address. After getting the paper from his colleague, the rabbi asked her what had happened. Reluctantly, she replied that after her guests had left, the police came and asked her many questions. Fear had replaced the smile on her face.

The Campaign of Spiritual Destruction

The Jew can survive economically in the Soviet Union, but he is treated like a second-class citizen. An American diplomat, a non-Jew, after three years of service in the U.S. embassy in Moscow, concluded that despite some token cultural and religious concessions in recent years, a fair observer would have to conclude that Soviet Jews represented the most underprivileged group in the Soviet Union, whether classified as a religious group, a nationality or both. One East European Jew I encountered told me that in most Communist countries, especially in the U.S.S.R., the authorities conduct a deliberate campaign aimed at the spiritual destruction of Jewish religious, cultural and social values and traditions by forcing them to wipe out their past. He said:

This is achieved by a systematic and carefully thought out psychic and economic pressure on Jewish inhabitants, especially when they are not ready to give up their Jewish identity. Various methods are used to foster a variety of anti-Semitism, from the artful and hidden to the open and brutal attack, all operated from special ideological departments closely co-operating with the secret police.

II
The Young Russian Jew

Nothing in our visit was more revealing, either as a subject for study or one for rueful contemplation, than the position of the young Russian Jew. He is reared in a Communist society where the Marxist philosophy of dialectical materialism invades every concept of ethics, humanism and religion, and opens its cornucopia of benefits to every Jew—provided he renounces his Judaism in all its aspects.

He may do so, indeed, but he must hurry, for unless he is the issue of an intermarriage, Soviet law requires that at the age of sixteen he must, like other nationalities, register and have his identity card clearly marked "Jew." Thereupon begins his indoctrination into the devious ways of discrimination—some subtle, some overt—in employment, schooling and cultural life-support.

This, as much as anything else, impels the Jewish youth to a seminal identity with Judaism in its broadest sense, as well as a striving for kinship with the State of Israel.

In his book, *The Jews of Silence*, Elie Wiesel says: "Young Jews in Russia want to return to Judaism, but without the slightest notion of the meaning of its mission. This is their tragedy."[1]

Few, indeed, are the Jewish families where some spark is not communicated from father to son. In Moscow, for instance, the young people do go to the Central Synagogue for the High Holy Days and Sukkos celebrations. They watch their fathers and grandfathers pray and kiss the Torah, the scroll containing the five Books of Moses; they attend vaudeville and entertainments given in Yiddish; they avidly admire the nationalistic fervor of Israel and they do try to learn the Hebrew language from every source at their command. As a salmon returns upstream to spawn, so does the young Russian Jew strive to reach backward. Rarely is he able to offer a simple, logical, unequivocal reason for the yearning.

Once, in a museum, a girl from Baku was attracted to us because a woman in our group was wearing a Star of David. We were eager to exchange information with the girl, who had rarely seen a foreigner and never a foreign Jew. Before we knew what had happened, a female official materialized from nowhere, took the girl brusquely by the arm and pulled her away. We watched as she lectured the youngster on the evils of speaking to strangers.

On another occasion, Rabbi and Mrs. Emmet Frank of Seattle, were approached by a Jewish teen-ager who had noticed the rabbi's El Al bag. The couple asked whether his parents attended the synagogue. The boy replied that his mother lighted candles nearly every Sabbath Eve and that both parents frequently went to services. Then, rather defensively, he said that he did not need Judaism for himself, because Communism was his inspiration. But when Mrs. Frank reached into her handbag and gave the boy a mezuzah, his eyes filled with tears. He kissed her hand, thanked her and looked about to see if anyone had witnessed the scene.

Geula Gill

Perhaps our most exilarating experience occurred in Leningrad. At a concert by Israeli folk singer Geula Gill, we encountered masses of young Russian Jews. The singer gave twenty-three concerts in several cities of the Soviet Union, each time to an audience of more than 2500, not including standees. The enthusiasm everywhere was so great that six additional concerts had to be arranged.

I heard about the concert tour upon reaching Moscow and was told that our arrival date in Leningrad would coincide with Miss Gill's final concert in that city. We asked Sergei to try and get tickets for the entire group. "Is possible," he replied. In Moscow and Vilna we reminded him and were assured he had cabled ahead for tickets. The day we arrived in Leningrad, again I asked Sergei about the tickets in the presence of two local Intourist guides, who were, as it happened, Jewish. The two guides claimed not to have heard of the show and took me to the hotel desk to check a list of entertainment events in the city. The men at the desk shrugged. "There is no such concert," they said. An hour later, a friend brought me ten tickets. The next day one of the two local guides, apparently forgetting herself, told a member of our party that she had tried to obtain tickets for her parents to the same unadvertised concert, only to be told that no more seats were available.

Eight of us arrived at the theater and found the lobby jammed with people looking for tickets. We were nearly mobbed when we gave one of our extra tickets to an old man and the other to a young Jewish engineer. We identified ourselves, and the older man said that many Jews in the community were aware of our presence because news of the visit had been announced on an overseas broadcast. The engineer expressed his admiration for Israel and told us that twice a year he attended synagogue services, unafraid of informers finding him in the large crowd. He said he used the concert as another way to declare his Jewishness. In describing his life in an assimilated society, he did not appear to be discontent, but did express a wish for some link with other Jews.

The packed auditorium erupted repeatedly with applause as the artist sang Yiddish, Hebrew and Israeli songs. She closed the concert with a moving rendition of "Eli, Eli" (My God, My God), which left many in the audience weeping. They refused to let her go and demanded scores of encores. The artist said later that during her first Moscow appearance she stepped down into the audience to shake hands with the people, who became so enthusiastic that they started to tear her clothing. Each of her shows was scheduled for forty-five minutes, but lasted two hours.

Afterward, we were followed with interest by several hundred young people. Rabbi Mihaly stood on the steps of the bus and described the rich and abundant Jewish life in the United States, and the numerous schools, youth groups, synagogues and fraternal organizations. Our new friends were reluctant to let us go and kept up the questions. Because we feared the authorities might step in and arrest us for conducting a meeting, we had the driver close the door. As the bus started to leave, some of the people asked for the name of our hotel and promised to meet us there the next day. They never came. We wondered whether they were unable to or were afraid.

In her reminiscences of the tour, the petite Israeli singer said each concert was an emotional experience. Miss Gill believed her appearance in the native land of her parents gave the Jews, who saw her, "strength and hope for twenty more years."

In the lobby of her hotel, young people waited hours for a chance to speak with her. She marveled at their beautiful pronunciation of Hebrew, which they had learned from dictionaries, books, recordings and listening to Kol Yisrael, the Israel Broadcasting Company.

Incident in Riga

A tragic incident occurred after Miss Gill's concert in Riga, capital of Soviet-occupied Latvia. Her enthusiastic reception, especially by young people, concerned the Soviet officials. Containment of liberal trends among all youth in the U.S.S.R. today has become the rule. Unfortunately, the Kremlin hierarchy misinterprets enthusiasm for rebellion.

Upon her arrival in Riga, the local concert manager

told Miss Gill that for her own protection she could no longer be permitted to mingle with the audience. Furthermore, he strongly advised she should return to her hotel after the performance and refrain from greeting admirers at the stage door. The artist noted the presence of an unusual number of policemen and military personnel, who she later learned had set up barricades against the crowd. After the concert, the manager ushered her and the other members of the troupe into a bus. An orchestra member tried to help her open a window so that, at least, she could satisfy some autograph seekers, but the windows were stuck. The crowd tried so hard to see her that one group pushed close to the bus and shut the door on the fingers of a musician. In the excitement, a fifteen-year-old girl attempted to get close to Miss Gill. She was stopped by a policeman who threw her back into the crowd and shouted, "Little Jew, go back!"

The girl slapped the man's face, and he arrested her. As others came to her defense, a second officer aided by a plainclothesman struggled with the crowd and arrested a twenty-three-year-old man who was later charged with attacking an officer. That night the police also arrested a forty-five-year-old Jewish woman and charged her with leading a delegation to the police station to free the girl. Three days later the authorities arrested her uncle, an engineer, who supposedly had assaulted an officer. The older woman was additionally charged with calling the policemen names, such as "anti-Semite" and "Gestapo agents." She is alleged to have exclaimed that she could not live in such a totalitarian environment and wanted to leave the Soviet Union. There was to have been a trial, but results were never officially announced. The girl and her uncle were released. The others, it was later learned, were each sentenced to two years in prison.

Immediately after the incident, the Central Committee of the Latvian Communist Party met and ordered a news blackout. It is said that sentences for the accused were determined at the same meeting. Foreign correspondents who learned of the affair and attempted to reach Riga were denied travel permits in Moscow.

Miss Gill told me afterward that Jews still came to her saying, "We can talk to you and do everything we like. We are not afraid." As they uttered these words, she said, their eyes expressed fear.

The Wish to Be a Jew

Two Western journalists, returning home after several years in Moscow, confirmed in conversation that a tremendous sense of Jewish pride exists in the average Russian Jew today, especially among the young. All they wish is to identify—not as religious Jews, but just as Jews.

There was an opportunity to hold a discussion at length with a Communist-reared youth from Czechoslovakia, on a student trip to the West. Until the beginning of Alexander Dubcek's liberal regime, Czechoslovakia was considered closest to the U.S.S.R. and to the Communist system in general.

The youth had stronger personal ties with Judaism

than most, since his father had been an inmate of a
Nazi concentration camp. After the shackling of Dubcek's
administration, he fled the Soviet occupation and now
attends a university elsewhere in Europe. Despite the
Russian take over, which jarred his adherence to socialism, he hopes one day to return to Prague and resume
his life there.

I asked the nineteen-year-old what Judaism meant to
him. His response was: "It does not mean for me religion. I have nothing against religion. I recognize from
the historical point of view that religion in America is
the strongest thing. With my peers, religion does not
play an important part; most of my friends are atheists
or agnostics, so why should I believe in religion? I am
curious about it, yes, and would like to learn about some
of the theological theories."

The young man's only exposure to Judaism had been
an occasional visit to the synagogue and some history
taught to him by his father. Like so many of his generation, the father had expressed guilt regarding the limited knowledge he could impart to his son.

The boy told of his first visit to the synagogue. "I
thought that Judaism in the Orthodox fashion is not for
me." (This visit, at the age of fifteen, occurred at a time
when he was trying, it appears, to find some way to
embrace Judaism.) He continued: "There exists no freedom for the child who has Orthodoxy forced upon him.
It is right for older people to enter into this voluntary
religious isolation, but why force the same on their children? Although there is a danger of assimilation on one

hand, it's better than the dogmatism of an Orthodox Jew."

During this introduction to organized worship, the youth remembered his incredulous reaction as his father translated the Hebrew prayers for him. "How could people worship something that doesn't exist?" he asked. The young man's Communist-indoctrinated education had helped destroy any chance of understanding that there can be a *rapprochement* between religion and science. He was more influenced by the doctrine of dialectic materialism than by belief in God. He rejected the concept of accepting anything as God-created, which science could not explain. "Perhaps some things will remain unknown to man. I don't know whether it's good to call this religion."

He expressed amazement at the survival of the Jewish people. "It's difficult to understand how the nation survived so many tragedies. Perhaps that's why so many Jews are religious. Personally, I can't say what accounts for these survivals, but just because I cannot see beyond it is no reason to call it 'religion.'"

In further conversation, it developed that he believed that the real criteria for ethical standards of behavior came from his friends, who set their own behavior code. How would he justify the sacrifice of another life for his own survival? I asked. "Suppose you had a broken leg and you saw a man drowning. What would you do?" He replied, "I guess I would probably jump in to save the person. If that individual drowned, I would go around all my life with the feeling that I could have saved somebody but didn't even try." I surprised him when I said, "This is the real meaning of religion, not only a belief in God, but in the value judgment which man practices. You have just affirmed one of the basic beliefs of Judaism."

"Even though I know Jews ascribe to these values," he said, "I would prefer to call them human." If religion could be defined in terms of humanism he might be able to believe in it, he concluded. This young Jew admitted that in the presence of non-Jews, strangely enough, he quickly defended criticism of Jews or Judaism. "But," he said, "I identify first as a Czech, then as a Jew."

I asked the standard question: "What happens when you get married?" He replied that although it was immaterial to him whether he wed outside his faith, he would insist his children receive knowledge of Judaism and learn to respect its heritage and traditions. He placed no value in Judaism as a religion, but moved by family background and his father's experiences in the war, lay great store in the historical and philosophical tenets of the Jewish people.

Thus, in personal commitment, one finds hope for the future. Still, if the state has its way, Judaism as a religion and a culture will disappear with the passage of time.

Once cannot hope to understand the Soviet Jewish problem, however, through exposure to isolated incidents. It is essential to take into account the history of the Jew in Russia, his involvement in the early days of the Revolution, the dreaded Stalin era, the economic trials and the various cultural and religious suppressions wrought by official and subtle acts by the state. Collectively, these items form a damning case against the Soviet Union's deliberate campaign of anti-Semitism.

III

The Seeds of Anti-Semitism

Optimism has always been a basic characteristic of the Jewish people, especially so in Russia where it became a necessary crutch during centuries of oppression.

The Eastern Church has persistently played an influential part in the lives of the Russian people and their rulers. Christian prelates despised the Jews even before the seventh century when the Jews successfully converted the pagan Khazar monarchs. In the tenth century, when Vladimir, Prince of Kiev, chose Christianity as the official religion, the church heads, then ensconced and secure, vowed never to allow Judaism to succeed again. The word "Zhid" became synonymous with hate, and the seeds of anti-Semitism were sown and propagated.

In the centuries that followed, the charge by the church that Jews were guilty of killing Christ became part of the national ethos. In 1648, disaster struck the Ukranian Jews who were flourishing under Polish rule, but were despised by the peasant Cossacks as moneylenders, tax collectors, landlords and alleged Christ-killers. The Cossack leader, Bogdan Chmielnitsky, led a 1½-year-long brutal and bloody raid during which his troops tortured and raped and murdered more than

300,000 Jews. This wholesale slaughter was surpassed in the annals of history only by the Nazi holocaust. Chmielnitsky is honored in the Ukraine today as a hero of the Soviet people.

The Romanoffs and the "Black Hundred"

The Romanoffs varied in their attitudes toward Jews. Even rulers who might have exercised tolerance trod cautiously for fear of arousing the church. In 1786, for example, Catherine II (the Great) helped Jews in White Russia and Lithuania to stave off economic ruin by getting the Senate to pass equitable trade laws. This brought an influx of Jewish merchants to Moscow, and local tradesmen bitterly protested the competition. She thereupon ordered Moscow's Jews to colonize new territories in the southern provinces. The southern provinces plus the recently annexed Polish provinces thus formed the Pale of Settlement, an enormous ghetto where most Russian Jews were forced to live until the early twentieth century.

From 1649 to 1881, six hundred restrictive laws were drawn up by the Tsars against the Jews. The despotic Nicholas I (Tsar, 1825–55), an arch reactionary, was responsible for half of them. The reign of Alexander II was known as the "period of the great reforms." His son, Alexander III (Tsar, 1881–94), however, reversed the policies of his father. He was influenced by the dictates of his teacher Pobiednostzev, an ultra-conservative fanatic and head of the Holy Synod, known for his hatred of Jews. The discontented peasantry was told that

Jews were to blame for their condition, and a historic wave of pogroms broke out in New Russia and the Ukraine. The May laws of 1882, even more so than before, deprived Jews of moving their homes or businesses. The laws also forbade Jews from conducting business on Sundays or Christian holidays.[1] In 1887, the strict quota systems were established for Jews entering high schools and universities. Jews were prohibited from practicing many trades in which they had previously engaged, and in 1889 the area of the already overcrowded Pale was reduced. During this period of economic and political oppression, Jewish nationalist groups formed, and Jews also joined existing revolutionary movements. The first large wave of emigration to the United States began, and the first settlers left for Palestine.

Nicholas II (Tsar, 1894–1917), the final Tsar, needed Jewish scapegoats even more than had his father. Growing discontent among an increasingly large segment of the population resulted in wholesale strikes and demonstrations, the latter frequently calling out armed troops. After economic and social life came to a halt in the October uprising of 1905, the Tsar consented to a manifesto permitting the formation of a representative Duma, or parliament. The first two Dumas were dissolved by Nicholas when they proved too liberal. The third Duma, elected in 1907, consisted mostly of rightists, many of whom were anti-Semitic reactionaries. This parliament, carrying out many dictates of the autocracy, adopted new and harsh measures against the Jews. The liberal representatives proposed that the Pale of Settlement be abolished, but the proposal was defeated by the rightist majority.

Nicholas then condoned and secretly subsidized the Facist "union of the Russian people," whose "Black Hundred" gangs launched a new wave of pogroms, beginning with the Kishinev pogrom in 1903, which left 45 people dead, 586 injured and 1500 houses and stores looted or demolished. A high point of these infamous campaigns was the staging of the now-famous blood-libel case of Mendel Beiliss from 1911 to 1913 (on which Bernard Malamud based his award-winning novel *The Fixer*), in which the authorities fabricated evidence that the accused had ritualistically murdered a nine-year-old Christian boy.

The Bund and the Zionists

Jewish socialist and Zionist groups became increasingly well organized despite police repression. In 1897, two important Jewish bodies were formed: the League of Jewish Workingmen of Lithuania, Poland and Russia (The Bund), and the World Zionist Organization, which, although founded by Theodor Herzl and Max Nordau, both Hungarians, obtained its chief "source of manpower and much of its spiritual and ideological energy . . . from Russian Jewry."[2]

Russian Jews distinguished themselves during World War I when 400,000 Jewish soldiers were in the ranks and 34,000 were decorated for bravery in combat. Instead of being praised for their patriotism, the Jews were accused of using patriotism to buy equal rights, and many innocent Jews were charged with espionage. Wounded soldiers were returned to the Pale, and families inside were denied permission to visit some still in service. Efforts were made to play down, or to censor, press reports of Jewish heroism. When the Jewish weekly newspaper *Novy Woskhod* recorded these acts in a special volume, *The War and the Jews*, it was shut down. This deliberate downgrading of Jews is still exemplified today on the outskirts of Kiev at Babi Yar where more than 70,000 Jews were massacred and buried in a mass grave during World War II, but where there is not a single marker.

Major Contributions

The centuries of hardships did not prevent Jews from making major contributions to their own development. The study of Torah and Talmud was a way of life. The rabbi was revered as a great scholar and leader of his community and flock. In the early 1700s in Podoli, the mystical sect called Hasidism was founded by Israel Baal-Shem Tov, "master of the [good] name." The same period produced a renowned rabbinic scholar, Elijah the Vilna Gaon (a Hebrew title meaning "his excellency," given to outstanding Jewish scholars). Hebrew and Yiddish grew as Jewish languages of faith and culture.

The Haskalah (Hebrew for enlightenment) was created by Moses Mendelsohn, the German Jew, and his disciples in the late eighteenth century to teach European culture to ghetto Jews. During the mid-nineteenth century, Russian Jews introduced secular ideas into their education and literature. The Haskalah opened up new horizons, which led to the modernization of the Jew living in the Pale, and after 1882 stimulated the rise of Jewish nationalism and socialism.

Even when the earth trembled for him, as it were, the Jew yielded to creative impulse. Russian Jews gave to the world outstanding Jewish scholarship, the humor of a Sholom Aleichem, the poignancy of a Sholom Asch or I. J. and I. B. Singer, the lyric poetry of a Chaim Nachman Bialik, the scientific genius of Chaim Weizmann and many more.

The Revolution

The overthrow of the Romanoffs in March 1917 drastically altered conditions for the Russian masses. The new provisional government eliminated social, religious and national differences. The proclamation issued by the new regime, declaring Jews the equal of all other citizens, came like a breath of fresh air to the impoverished people of the Pale. Jewish optimism burst forth again. They invested their meager savings in the new government bonds. In Odessa alone, the Jewish community purchased thirty million rubles' worth.[3] Young men now able to enter military colleges quickly took advantage of their new status. Schools in Hebrew and Yiddish flourished, and political parties asserted themselves by protesting the treatment of fellow Jews in Rumania.

Jewish students in European universities were ripe for conversion to socialist universalism, to the philosophies of capitalism and industrialization, but also to the principle of democratic freedom for the emancipated proletariat.[4] Many found fulfillment as Jews in Zionism. Jews who had previously been affiliated with such Russian movements as Populism, which was prepared to use terror to overthrow the monarchy, now preferred to work through social-democratic organizations which disapproved of political assassination.

Lenin Against the Bund

In September 1897 in Vilna, when the Bund (the League), using Yiddish and Hebrew in its propaganda campaigns, was formed, success was immediate in spreading Western concepts of social democracy.[5] Aware that its membership outpolled the Russian revolutionaries three to one, the Bund, at the Second Congress of the Russian Social Democratic Party held in London on August 14, 1903, demanded autonomy. Determined, however, to create a single-party unit, Lenin rejected the idea of separate Jewish and Russian groups. The Bund believed that the party spoke only for a broad base of workers who eventually would assume the control from the *bourgeoisie*. Lenin felt that the party should be controlled by an elite corps of professionals guiding the workers along the path to social emancipation. The independent posture of the Bundists and the difference in basic philosophy caused a break at the congress meeting, splitting the party into Bolsheviks and Mensheviks. The Bund became part of the latter.

The Beginnings of Bolshevik Nationalism

The Jewish revolutionary who threw himself into the cause could not foresee that Bolshevism was developing into a new kind of nationalism with which he was bound to clash. Some observers consider that the wholesale commitment to the latter cause contributed to overtones of anti-Semitism, which became a recurrent feature of Bolshevism in later years, especially as developed by Stalin. Dr. Chaim Weizmann, a Russian who found a haven in Zionism, cautioned his brethren in July 1917, not to forget the warnings of history. The future first president of Israel warned: "Great hopes were raised by the French Revolution, also. The principles of equality may be decreed by law, but they take a considerable time before they become an integral part of the life of a nation. It is difficult to believe that anti-Semitism, which has been systematically urged and cruelly practiced in Russia for so long, will suddenly disappear."[6]

On November 7, 1917, the Bolsheviks, led by Vladimir Ilyich Lenin, seized power. Jews saw some of their own, such as Lev Davidovich Bronstein (Leon Trotsky), in the top ranks of the Communist government and anticipated that their new status would now flourish. Others were aware that Jewish party members identified with Judaism only in name, and had long given up environment and tradition in favor of the assimilation and atheism demanded by Marxist philosophy. Trotsky, when asked whether he considered himself a Jew or a Russian, said: "Neither, I am a social democrat, and that is all!"[7]

Although Jews were both leaders and followers in the ranks of Bolshevik revolutionaries, most, like Trotsky, had long ago rejected Jewish identity, leading Dr. Louis Greenberg, a prominent Jewish historian, to declare that "while the Jewish masses as the greatest sufferers of the Tsarist regime readily joined the ranks of the revolution and made significant contributions to its cause, the chief thinkers and leaders of the revolution were non-Jews."[8]

Lenin's Nationality Thesis

The Bolshevik Party's definition that Russian Jews did not constitute a nationality group within the new system served as the basis for the regime's subsequent Jewish policies. As long ago as 1903, Lenin had posed the question of Jewish loyalty, stating, in an article, "the Jewish question is this exactly: Assimilation or separateness? The idea of a Jewish 'nationality' is manifestly reactionary, not only when put forward by its consistent partisans (the Zionists), but also when put forward by those who try to make it agree with the ideas of Social Democracy (the Bundists). The idea of a Jewish nationality is in conflict with the interests of the Jewish proletariat for, directly or indirectly, it engenders in its ranks a mood hostile to assimilation, a 'ghetto' mood."[9]

Lenin's thesis was based on the views of Karl Kautsky, a leading interpreter of Marxist doctrines who greatly influenced the Bolshevik leader. This became evident when Lenin echoed Kautsky's definition of a nationality

group as having a common language and territory.
". . . Jewish national culture is the slogan of rabbis and
bourgeoisie, the slogan of our enemies. Anyone directly or
indirectly putting forward the slogan of Jewish national
culture is (whatever his good intentions) an enemy of
the proletariat, a partisan of the old and castelike in
the Jewish group. Those Jewish Marxists who merge with
Russian, Lithuanian, Ukrainian and other workers in international Marxist organizations, contributing their
share (in both Russian and Yiddish) to the creation of
an international culture of the labor movement—those
Jews carry on (in defiance of the separatism of the Bund)
the best Jewish tradition when they combat the slogan
of national culture."[10]

According to Dr. Solomon M. Schwarz, a former rank-
ing official in the provisional government, Lenin's position added up to the Jewish group being "neither a
nation or a nationality, but a caste; and, in the interest
of social progress, all castes must be destroyed. Insofar
as the Jewish question is one of oppression and discrimination, the establishment of racial and national equality
will solve that problem."[11]

Stalin echoed Lenin's view that Jews lacked both a
continuous territory and an argicultural base to qualify
as a national group, even though he conceded they did
possess "a common national character." He believed a
nation to be "a historically evolved stable community
formed on the basis of a common language, territory,
economic life and psychological make-up manifested in
a common culture."[12]

A former leading member of the British Communist Party, Dr. Hyman Levy, contended that Soviet authorities had made a false analysis of the Jewish problem. In 1958, Professor Levy, a distinguished scientist and mathematician, and professor emeritus of the University of London, outlined his challenge in an essay, "Jews and the National Question."

. . . a nation can never be defined, only an abstraction is capable of definition, and the Jews are by no means an abstraction. They are alive, active and virile. Any attempt to define a Jew, therefore, is philosophic nonsense. An international people cannot be eliminated by a national policy, it can only be wounded.[13]

These views eventually brought about Dr. Levy's expulsion from the party. Despite such questioning, the Lenin-Stalin evaluation has held firm in guiding the Kremlin's Jewish policies to this day.

Decree of the Council of People's Commissars

Almost immediately after their rise to power, the Bolsheviks were confronted with anti-Semitism by counterrevolutionaries in territories not under Bolshevik control. As Austrian and German armies evacuated the Ukraine and Byelorussia, the "White" forces, including the Tsar's Cossacks, ravaged the countryside in bitter combat with the Red armies.

Jews became the victims. The White Army was credited with carrying out 1520 pogroms in 911 cities and villages, resulting in 200,000 Jews killed and 700,000 wounded.[14] The counterrevolutionaries had cleverly identified Jews with the Bolsheviks and spread the gospel. Lenin saw that the anti-Semitism could serve to divide the masses. Furthermore, the new regime had won favor in the West by proving that wherever they were in control, Jew-baiting and pogroms ended. Once again, expediency, rather than doctrine, became the cardinal rule.

Therefore, on July 27, 1918, *Izvestia* published an official document called, *Decree by the Council of the People's Commissars for the Radical Suppression of the Anti-Semitic Movement*, drafted by Yakov Mikhailovich Sverdlov, one of the five Jewish deputies in the commissariat:

According to reports reaching the Council of People's Commissars, the counterrevolutionists are conducting a pogrom agitation in many cities, especially at the front border, with the result that excesses have been perpetrated in many places against the toiling Jewish masses.

The bourgeois counterrevolution is taking over into its hands the weapon which fell out of the Czar's hand. Whenever the autocratic government found it necessary to divert the wrath of the people away from itself, it directed this against the Jews. The Jewish rich always managed to find protection for themselves; the victims slain in the incitement and violence were the Jewish poor.

. . . In the Russian Soviet Federated Republic, where the principle of the self-determination of the toiling masses of all peoples has been proclaimed, there can be no place for national suppression. The Jewish bourgeois is our enemy not as a Jew but as a bourgeois; the Jewish toiler is our brother. Any incitement against any nation is intolerable, criminal and contemptible.

The Council of People's Commissars declare that the anti-Semitic movement and the pogroms on Jews are destructive to the cause of the workers' and peasants' revolution, and calls upon the toiling people of Socialist Russia to fight with all means against this evil.

Lenin personally added a last paragraph in red ink to strengthen the document:

The Council of People's Commissars orders all Soviet departments to take decisive means to destroy at the root the anti-Semitic movement. The pogromists and pogrom agitators must be placed outside the law.[15]

This document is the only pronouncement against anti-Semitism ever produced by the U.S.S.R.

Communist Attempts at Conversion

Despite the fact that many Jews were in the party hierarchy, Jewish masses had not yet been converted to Communist philosophy. The task of changing this confronted the Division of Jewish National Affairs, a section of the People's Commissariat for National Affairs, established under Stalin in January 1918. Publications in Yiddish, and local organizations, had to be created to extol the virtues of Communism. Personnel was difficult to recruit. Semen M. Dimanshtein, the new Jewish commissar, confessed to the first conference of Jewish sections in October 1918: ". . . those who undertook this work were not familiar with the Jewish workers' life, and some could not even speak Yiddish."[16] To augment the administrative function of the commissariat, the party flew in the face of its principles by establishing the Yevsektsia—Jewish sections of the Communist Party—to woo and recruit Jews. In January 1919, a Jewish Communist Party of White Russia was organized. Lenin's earlier argument against such separate enclaves was forgotten for the sake of expediency. "Time and again the party made concessions to the idea of Jewish autonomy, only to take them back when they had served their purpose," according to Dr. Solomon Schwarz.[17]

Jewish political structures in opposition had to be eliminated. In 1919, 1200 Zionist chapters, with a total membership of 300,000, were outlawed. Three thousand Zionist leaders were deported or sent to political labor camps.

Only some non-political organizations such as the Organization for Rehabilitation and Training (ORT) and the Jewish Colonization Association were permitted to retain their ties, since they received foreign funds and equipment to assist in the resettlement of Russian Jews dispersed after the war. Seventy-five per cent of these refugees had been tradesmen or businessmen who needed to be retrained as agricultural or factory workers. Many spoke only Yiddish: They lacked industrial skills and practiced ethnic and religious customs at odds with the new Soviet society.

Some funds for such efforts came from Western Jewish agencies convinced that their brethren had at last been emancipated. Both the Joint Distribution Committee and ORT helped set up schools for tractor building, shoemaking, farming and the manufacture of clothing, electrical tools and toys. Jewish officials soon learned these programs hardly aided the perpetuation of Jewish life, but rather the Communist goal of total integration and assimilation. On a visit to Moscow, a JDC delegation asked a Jewish foreman how many trainees in the program were Jews. He replied, "It's unimportant to be Jewish. The only thing that counts is whether you do good work."[18]

The urgency of special attention for the Jews soon faded as a party priority. By 1921 the Jewish commissariat had been demoted to the status of a department, which in April 1924, was dissolved. Thereafter, Jewish matters were handled by local officials.

Birobidzhan—a Jewish Homeland in Siberia?

On November 17, 1926, Soviet President Mikhail I. Kalinin offered a solution to the Jewish problem by recommending the creation of a Jewish national homeland on Russian soil. He envisioned this project as aiding the development of agrarianism and industrialization. Kalinin hoped that as a result hundreds of thousands of Jews would become part of a growing agriculture peasantry. "Only on this condition can the Jewish masses hope for the survival of their nationality,"[19] he proclaimed.

The site chosen was the far eastern Siberian wasteland of Birobidzhan, twice the size of New Jersey, consisting almost entirely of virgin forest and swampland, without roads, and virtually uninhabited. The plan almost immediately became a complete failure. Had the Communist recruiters appealed to the Jewish spirit of nationalism, and had they evangelized Jewish youth, the plan might have succeeded despite hardships. Fanning the flames of Jewish nationalism hardly constituted a Communist objective at the time, however.

A visitor in 1959 found so little evidence of Jewish occupancy that street signs were not to be found in Yiddish; the language was not taught in schools; there were no Yiddish films or books generally available; and the thrice-weekly newspaper, *Birobidzhaner Stern*, had a circulation of only 1000 and consisted mainly of reprinted stories from *Izvestia* and *Pravda*.

The regime, in wishing to segregate Jews and to develop an industrial and agricultural colony in the bargain, had forgotten to alter the extreme cold of winter and the oppressive heat of summer. When Jews, who were not especially imbued with pioneer zeal in the direction of Birobidzhan, heard reports of the uncompromising weather, their resettlement attitude was something like "Thanks, but no thanks."

Still, the regime was intent on the idea of a Jewish state and the favorable impression it was bound to make upon foreign Jews. The remade Birobidzhan was also sure to attract considerable financial aid for welfare and training programs, for development of the region's dormant and natural resources, and for erecting a buffer against Japanese aggression and immigrant Chinese infiltration.

Stalin's Purges

Then came Joseph Stalin (Dzhugashvili), the shoemaker's son from Gori, near Tbilisi, in Georgia.

"To him will fall the glory of being the greatest criminal in history. . . . Every crime was possible to Stalin, for there was not one he had not committed." So Milovan Djilas described Joseph Stalin after a number of conversations with the Kremlin leader. The Yugoslav writer and former vice-president said, "In him was joined the criminal senselessness of a Caligula with the refinement of a Borgia and the brutality of Tsar Ivan the Terrible."[20]

For the Russian Jew, Stalin's twenty-nine-year rule represented a period of terror and death, which most had assumed could not happen again. In an essay on the nationality question, the Soviet Premier had set a virtual deadline for the disappearance of Russian Jewry. They were to cease to exist after the Pale had been abolished.[21] All about him, the dictator saw a viable, though Communist-oriented Jewish culture, with Jews continuing to exist and to grow as a people.[22]

In 1930, Stalin ordered the abolishment of the Jewish affairs department, commonly known as the Yevsekstia, and between 1936–38 removed most of the remaining Jewish Communists from top echelons of government. Such figures as Semen M. Dimanshtein, Alexander Chemeriskii, Maria Y. Frumkina, Grigory E. Zinoviev, Lev B. Kamenev and Karl Radek were executed or exiled. Thus, in 1939, when Stalin consummated his "time-saving" pact with Hitler, he might have pleased his new ally by pointing to the dilution and stagnation of Jewish life in the U.S.S.R.

The Red Army, upon taking control of the Baltic states and part of Poland, immediately closed Jewish schools, research organizations, and philanthropic and mutual-aid societies. Jewish leaders and intellectuals were jailed, exiled or executed. One of the most renowned Jewish publishing houses, the Widow and Brothers Rom of Vilna, capital of Soviet-occupied Lithuania, producers of sacred Talmudic folios and literature, was demolished. Russian soldiers ransacked the premises, destroyed type and book plates, and dismantled all remaining usable equipment and shipped it to Moscow.

The climate shifted somewhat when the Kremlin anticipated the Nazi attack. All citizens were needed now in the war effort. Internally, Jews had to be provided with a sense of national pride, while their brethren outside Russia had to continue swallowing the propaganda disseminated by Western Communist and front organizations that the land of the proletariat was a champion of all minorities, a leader in the struggle against Hitlerism and a "paradise for Jews."

The Revival of Pride

But Stalin had destroyed most of the leaders and vehicles of such a campaign. How to revive a Jewish consciousness after stifling it? In September 1941, two Polish Jews who had been released by the Red Army, Victor Alter and Henryk Ehrlich, outlined a blueprint for the establishment of a Jewish anti-Fascist committee whose purpose would be to assist Jews in Nazi-occupied Europe and to mobilize international Jewry to aid in the fight against the Germans. At the suggestion of Lavrenti Beria, head of the NKVD (Soviet secret police), the two Jews drafted the plans and gave copies to both Beria and Stalin.

As soon as the ink was dry, both men were executed, but on April 8, 1942, Solomon A. Lozovsky, chief of the Soviet Information Bureau, announced the formation of the Jewish Anti-Fascist Committee, supported and staffed by leading Soviet Jewish artists, writers, scientists, intellectuals and members of other professions. Yiddish writers were told that they no longer needed to adhere to Communist insistence to reject any part of their Jewish past. The Soviets provided the Jewish writer with an opportunity to open his heart and express an inner emotion suppressed for too long. Once again, many Jews considered that this represented a new chapter in the regime's Jewish posture. The feeling of Jewishness became so strong that the man in the street believed something was changing. Itzik Feffer, an officer of the new Anti-Fascist Committee and a prominent writer, whose verse lauding the Grand Mufti's terror against Palestinian Jews had just been completed, now switched, and in his poem, *I Am a Jew*, referred to the revolts of the Maccabees and the Zionist chants of the twelfth-century Hebrew poet Yehuda Halevi.

The best example of a writer who changed was the late Ilya Ehrenburg. During the war he hesitatingly accepted membership in the Anti-Fascist Committee and went on the air urging fellow Jews to remember their Jewishness. He asked Jews captured by the Nazis to wear the yellow Star of David as a mark of glory. Some sources say that after the war he informed on members of the Anti-Fascist Committee when he saw the trend of Stalinist actions. Shortly thereafter, in 1948, he publicly argued with Israeli Ambassador Golda Meir at a reception when he debated with her the concept of Jewish peoplehood and denounced this view as being contrary to Marxist-Leninist doctrines. He further emphasized that Russian Jews had no relationship with their brethren in other lands.

The Nazi Threat

However, despite a stepped-up pro-Jewish campaign during World War II, the Soviet press made little preparation to warn the Jews of their danger at the hands of the Nazis. During my visit to Vilna in 1966 a leader of the Jewish community there confirmed this. He said, "We heard about none of the German atrocities, and most of us thought it would be like it was under the kaiser's occupation, that we would receive better treatment by the Germans than by the Russians." In this Lithuanian city, where the Nazis destroyed almost the entire Jewish population, thousands of Jews were prevented from crossing the Lithuanian-Russian border by Red border guards only three days before the Germans arrived in the city.

In his book, *The Kremlin, the Jews and the Middle East*, Dr. Judd Teller relates disturbing accounts of anti-Semitism among the Red Army and partisan guerrillas. The latter, Dr. Teller reports, often showed greater zest for massacring Jews than for waging the war. His case histories were based on documentation provided by former partisans, including Jechiel Granatsztein, now an Israeli citizen; Shmerek Kaczerginski, and a former Red Army colonel, Vasili Yershov, now a United States citizen. One incident describes the case of a woman, attached to the 66th Group who talked back to her superior officer, a bitterly anti-Semitic commander, who had her executed after a five-minute trial. Another tells about a partisan raid upon a Nazi collaborator's wedding party, which they thought included many Nazi officers. Not finding any Nazis the raiders looted and ransacked the house. Sonya, a Jewish guerrilla, stripped a pair of silk stockings from the bride, whom the group commander promptly claimed for his mistress. Two weeks later the partisans returned, and before the assembled villagers an officer read Sonya's court martial verdict for "conduct unbecoming a partisan" and had her shot in front of the assemblage. A third incident is related about a band of ghetto escapees who had formed a Jewish unit behind the lines. Kolya Wochonin, a jealous commander of another group, decided to eliminate the Jewish "rivals" by staging a surprise raid upon their camp. He killed most of them.

Numerous incidents of Russian citizens and police officers aiding the Nazis in ferreting out and rounding up Jews were related after the war. But the most blatant act of all occurred in a ravine outside of Kiev, where, aided by Ukrainians, 70 thousand to 100 thousand Jews were herded and shot at Babi Yar. One wonders how people would have felt had they overheard Stalin tell Polish exile General Anders, an avowed anti-Semite, that he agreed with him not to include Jews in his Polish army since they were notoriously poor soldiers. During

World War II, 132,822 Jews received decorations by the Russians for heroism at the front.[23]

The Annihilation of Culture

As the war ended, authorities clamped down on Jewish cultural activities. "A new secular Yiddish culture and literature was demanded," Dr. Yehoshua Gilboa, Israeli journalist and victim of the Stalin era, told me. "Once again the commissars insisted that writers eliminate the Jewish past and only produce literature in the ideological framework of the Communist system." Although some people complied for fear of the consequences, many refused. Stalin recognized that once the emotional fervor of the Jew was aroused, it was hard to dampen. Stern measures had to be enacted if his plan for Russification of Jews was to become a reality.

The war, of itself, had already reduced most Jewish cultural facilities. Schools and historical institutions were closed, and most of the Yiddish type in the nation's printing presses had been melted down. Very few periodicals remained, among them the thrice-weekly periodical *Einigkeit* of the Anti-Fascist Committee; a few volumes published in the Ukraine, two volumes of a three-volume edition of a Yiddish almanac and the Birobidzhaner *Stern*.

Stalin's campaign of annihilation began with Jews portrayed in Soviet media as obstructionists, wartime slackers, black marketeers and Zionist spies. Charges of "cosmopolitanism" and bourgeois maintenance of ties with foreigners became synonymous with the word "Jew."

The campaign continued as, in October 1948, the secret police closed down the offices of the Anti-Fascist Committee for allegedly being "a center of subversion." Similar actions were taken against Emes, the only Jewish publishing house, and the Jewish State Theatre. Terror hovered in the air as Jewish cultural leaders slept with small bags under their pillows, prepared to flee at a moment's notice, to escape arrest. (Fig. 1) Stalin practiced a morbid joke on the Yiddish poet Peretz Markish, a co-chairman with Feffer of the Anti-Fascist Committee, when he ordered police to take him in the middle of the night to the Kremlin to honor him with a medal. Later, both Markish and Feffer were seized, and during the summer of 1952, were tried and executed. On August 12, 1952, 26 of the best-known Jewish poets and novelists were shot. During the four-year span from 1948 to 1952, 238 writers, 87 artists, 99 actors and 19 musicians, totaling 443 leaders of Jewish culture, died by execution, torture or from hardships.[24]

Stalin's phobia about the Jewish threat to his regime reached unparalleled heights in the following months. He began worrying about the Semitic connections of those close to him: Marshall Voroshilov was married to a woman of Jewish extraction, Kaganovich was a Jew, Molotov's wife was a Jew, Beria's mother was half Jewish, and Khrushchev's daughter was married to a Jewish journalist. This was more than he could bear. He set about implementing a fanatical plan to cleanse the nation of Jews by transporting them to some region far in the north, where they could die quickly of cold and starvation.[25]

On January 13, 1953, Soviet newspapers carried the announcement that nine Russian doctors, six of them Jews and all physicians in the Kremlin, had confessed to plotting the elimination of Soviet military and political leaders. They were blamed for the deaths of Andrei Zhdanov and Alexander Shcherbakov, former leading members of the Politburo. The physicians were linked with the American Jewish Joint Distribution Committee, which was accused of being an "international Jewish bourgeois nationalist organization . . . under the guidance of the American intelligence service, conducting wide-scale espionage, terroristic and other subversive activities in a number of countries, including the Soviet Union." The distinguished medical men allegedly confessed to being "secret enemies of the people, subjecting their patients to injurious treatment and undermining their health." In an editorial following this announcement, *Pravda* said of the JDC, "The exposure of the gang of physician-poisoners is a blow to the international Zionist organization."

According to the London *Jewish Chronicle*, it was the first time Moscow had used the labels "Jewish" and "Zionist" in the denunciation of crimes.[26] Harrison Salisbury, former New York *Times* correspondent to Moscow, reported the account as "chilling my blood. Those accused doctors have been the most respected and honored in the Soviet medical profession. This is serious business, very serious business. No one who read the item—the simple workmen who crowded around *Pravdas* pasted on billboards or the diplomats in their comfortable chancelleries—could fail to realize how important it is."[27]

In the United States, the JDC quickly rejected the accusation as "fantastic" and its chairman, Edward M. Warburg, said: "We categorically deny that there is any truth whatsoever in any of these charges." Predictably, the Soviet Union broke diplomatic relations with Israel on February 12, 1953. One year later, Salisbury described the Doctors' Plot as a "paranoiac conspiracy" and remembered the fear of most foreign correspondents in Moscow as they witnessed wholesale arrests, wondering if they themselves might not be next.

The Death of Stalin

Late in February 1953, Stalin was said to have summoned Communist Party presidium members to the Kremlin. Because of an alleged "Zionist and imperialist" plot against the Soviet Union and him, he planned to deport all Russian Jews to Birobidzhan, 3800 miles east of Moscow. At this disclosure, a heavy silence fell. Then Kaganovich asked Stalin whether this included every single Jew. The leader assured him that a "certain selection" would be made. Foreign Minister Vyacheslav Molotov, in a trembling voice, suggested that such a move would have a deplorable effect upon world opinion. At this point, Marshal Voroshilov threw his party card on the table and cried, "If such a step is taken I would be ashamed to remain a member of our party, which will be completely dishonored." Stalin flew into a rage and shouted at Voroshilov, "Comrade Kliment, it is I who will decide when you no longer have the right to keep your membership card." Suddenly, Stalin fell to the floor, unconscious. Ironically, fifteen minutes passed before doctors could be summoned, since the dictator's personal physicians were imprisoned after the alleged Doctors' Plot. Stalin never recovered and died on March 5, 1953. This version of Stalin's death was related by Panteleimon K. Ponomarenko, the Soviet ambassador to Poland, to Polish correspondents in Warsaw early in 1957. It was then told to a correspondent of the French newspaper, *France-Soir,* and subsequently reported in the New York *Times.*[28]

Eventually, the doctors and some of their coreligionists were released from prison or posthumously rehabilitated, and diplomatic relations with Israel were resumed. The full story of the Stalin horror and how it existed for so long has yet to be accurately recorded. In Djilas's words, "Until precisely this is explained by Stalin's present critics—I mean his successors—they will only confirm that in good part they are only continuing his work and that they contain in their own make-up those same elements— the same ideas, patterns, and methods that propelled him."[29] Today, after more than fifty years of Communist rule, we see that numerous physical and personal changes have been wrought for the benefit of most Soviet citizens. What has it brought for the Jews?

IV
Anti-Semitism Today

A glow of hope radiated over the worn, haggard faces as worshipers overflowing Moscow's Central Synagogue grabbed the hands of their Western visitors to exchange a *"Gut Shabbos"* (Good Sabbath) greeting.

An old man with a flowing white beard held my sleeve tightly, hoping I would linger to exchange a friendly word. As I placed my hand on his cheek in acknowledgment, he smiled, understanding that we had to take our places in the front pews set aside as a friendly "ghetto," surrounded by trusted members of the congregation.

As I sat down, sadness tightened my throat and nearly prevented me from whispering to a member of our group, "We've just come from viewing the remnants at Auschwitz, but to me this is a living Auschwitz."

The congregation looked like an old-age home. These elderly Jews, some of the last defenders of their faith in Russia, were a depressing sight for any visitor to the Soviet Union. Yet, if one was at all attuned to their problems, one could not escape this encounter with reality.

Despite the indifference of their own children to the past, they were experiencing the rigors of anti-Semitism in a society where, at best, they constituted second-class citizens.

Religious Jews in the Soviet Union represent Orthodoxy —old-fashioned and unchanging. As Rabbi Israel Miller, past chairman of the American Jewish Conference on Soviet Jewry, explained, "Although they haven't kept up with the times, in terms of the social issues of the day it is unimportant. In Russia it's the only synagogue that exists." This American Orthodox spiritual leader encountered the same noises and conversations throughout the service during his trip to the Soviet Union as we had. "It was more like the kind of Orthodoxy I knew as a child. I never heard such a tumult in the synagogue during the reading of the Torah. If this were to happen in my own congregation, I would rise in righteous indignation and call them to order.

"However," he said, "this is the only opportunity they have to speak to each other as Jews. They're not afraid, because they are in a large group; there's a certain anonymity."

Sabbath at Central Synagogue in Moscow

We returned the following morning to participate in the Sabbath with our coreligionists. Two sections of pews were set aside for visitors during the peak tourist season, on the right-hand side down front and on the pulpit. Those surrounding the guests would smile and engage in friendly exchanges, always volunteering: "We have no problems. Life here is good for us."

If a visitor were able to hide among the worshipers, he

Figure 1. Get out! Parasite from Moscow.

ИЗВЕСТИЯ

СОВЕТОВ ДЕПУТАТОВ ТРУДЯЩИХСЯ СССР

№ 270 (14740)
Год издания 48-й

Четверг, 12 ноября 1964 г.

Цена 2 коп.

— Рекомендую — отличное оружие! Проверено, опробовано и пристреляно в Освенциме, в варшавском гетто...

Рис. В. Фомичева.

Figure 2. The pattern for Soviet propaganda attacks was laid much earlier in this cartoon published in the national edition of the government's official organ on November 12, 1964. It shows the Nazi general holding a blood-dripping weapon with the caption: "I recommend this excellent weapon. It's been checked, tested and fired at Auschwitz." The accompanying article attacked an Israeli-West German arms deal.

Figure 3. Dayan to Hitler: Move on!

Figure 4. "Compass" of American-British manufacture.

was ferreted out by trusted synagogue elders and politely, but firmly, ushered to where the other visitors were. Once, a member of our group, Rabbi Albert Plotkin of Phoenix, succeeded in sitting at the back, and an older man whispered to him in Yiddish, "When they ask you where you're from, tell them Vilna." We were in for a worship service that lasted five hours.

A cantor from Tashkent, flown in for our benefit, filled the synagogue with loud, clear tones as he sang the liturgical music. On a pulpit chair at the side of the *bima* (pulpit), which was lighted with neon lights, sat Rabbi Levin, Moscow's only rabbi, an old and tired man; yet, as one woman described him, "with a beautiful, compassionate face, large pale-blue eyes over an aquiline nose, and a well-kept, flowing gray beard." The synagogue showed the need for repairs. Two small stained-glass windows above the ark were broken, the chandeliers were covered with layers of dust, and paint cans and ladders were strewn about the courtyard.

Rabbi Weinstein of our group spoke in Yiddish of the universal Jewish emphasis on peace and the need to curb nuclear armaments, and reminded the congregants that many American rabbis stemmed from the Pale of Settlement. He was followed by Dr. Mihaly who recounted the great scholarly traditions and contributions to Jewish learning made by Russian Jews.

A final message in Russian by Russian-born Rabbi Lieberman told the attentive worshipers that America's almost six million Jews and their Soviet brethren were united by common history, spiritual heritage, religious ideals and mankind's hope for the future.

"We have not forgotten you. You live in our loving thoughts," he said. Rabbi Levin's price for permitting foreign guests to address his flock, as on similar occasions, became evident as he pleaded for us to tell the American people: "End the bloodshed in Vietnam; use your influence to establish peace; do what you can to end the war."

The most emotional moment for all came during the Torah-reading portion of the service, thanks to one of the three teen-agers in our group. Many of the rabbis had been given aliyas (honors to recite the Torah blessing), including Rabbi Lieberman's thirteen-year-old son, David, who had celebrated his *bar mitzvah* only a month earlier. "As my brother stepped up to the pulpit, the men and women were still extremely noisy," his older sister, Debbie, recalled. "Suddenly, when everyone noticed a young boy, a hush fell over the worshipers. They all came forward and crowded around the pulpit. It was so quiet that David's small voice rang true and clear in the women's gallery upstairs." Mrs. Lieberman remembered the women hanging over the balcony railing to get a glimpse of her son, visible with his red velvet yarmulke (skull cap) as he chanted the Hebrew prayer. Several cried, *"Der yingle, der yingle"* (the young one). David expressed a sense of rebirth to these people. This was the first time in forty years that a youngster had participated in a service in the Moscow synagogue.

David voiced his own reaction to the experience: "As I turned around, the men started to close in on me, most of them were crying, and for a while I thought I'd be crushed. I noticed the tears in their eyes as they pressed forward. They just wanted to touch me and kiss my hand. After the service the women came down, and many kissed me. It was very moving, but also quite upsetting and depressing."

Afterward, the old women in the gallery, which was only one-tenth full, became more trusting. One of them readily confessed that "discrimination does exist against Jews. Only a small percentage go to the university, and then only if they can afford a bribe."

One of them said there were informers among the congregants who reported on the others, that even the women's gallery had its watchdogs. "One doesn't live here; we just exist," another volunteered. Many expressed amazement when told that thousands of Jewish children attend religious schools in the United States. "The news that somewhere in the world Judaism is being taught and studied, and that a young life perpetuates the heritage of his parents, seemed to serve for many as an encouraging sign," Mrs. Lieberman said. Many women were impressed by the youthfulness of the rabbis and their wives. As Mrs. Lieberman waited downstairs with the other American women for the kiddush reception to which Rabbi Levin had invited us, a man approached her and in perfect English asked, "How do you like the service? What do you think of Russia?" Another rabbi's wife, standing nearby, heard a male worshiper whisper in her ear in Yiddish, "Don't trust him, he's an informer."

The kiddush table was laden with freshly baked bread, sardines, cucumbers, tomatoes, apricots, vodka, brandy and soda. The reception provided an opportunity for Rabbi Levin to meet privately with his guests. However, he was surrounded by the same lay officials who, on other occasions, intone Soviet policy to foreigners. We asked Rabbi Levin, "What can we do for you?" He answered, "If you are familiar with Russian Jews, why ask what help we need?" He then recited a familiar line, "We need nothing, we have the right to open a Yeshiva (rabbinic seminary), but alas, we have no students. New prayer books are ready for publication; only the paper grant awaits approval."

Worship at Other Synagogues

Experiences in the synagogues grew steadily more depressing. In Vilna, a few of us left a propaganda film to attend the evening service at the only remaining Jewish house of worship in that city, once a world-famous center of Jewish learning and scholarship. Inside the sanctuary with its boarded-up windows, we surprised the handful of people present, who were barely enough for a minyan (a quorum of ten men required for traditional synagogue services). The bewildered and somewhat frightened worshipers welcomed us to join their prayers, and, after services, asked if we knew relatives of theirs in America or Israel. As we were leaving, we noticed two men in dark business suits approaching. No doubt existed in our minds whom they represented. They were there to question the Jews about our visit. The following day our itinerary included the same synagogue for what our Intourist guide hoped would be, "a short stop, yes?" Upstairs we discovered three rooms filled with incomplete Torah scrolls, Megilot (The Book of Esther) and prayer books. Most were in shabby condition, covered with layers of dust. As we examined a Torah scroll wrapped in an old, dirty, threadbare Soviet flag, the shamos (sexton) told us that these treasures had been rescued from the Nazis by a priest during the war. A great many of the books were Talmudic editions from the Widow Rom Press, whose famous printing plant had been demolished by the Red Army on the march to Poland. No indemnification has been offered by the U.S.S.R. to replace this scholarly treasure.

At the Leningrad synagogue, we met a group of British and Italian furriers, regular worshipers there during their annual trip to the fur auction. They told us that a new wave of fear had swept the congregation, and that recently members had been arrested or intimidated by the authorities. There was little doubt that visitors were purposely separated from the congregants when the women in our group reported that they had been crowded into a newly built "guest pen," a Formica-covered partition, cordoning off a section of the first two rows with only a small door as an exit.

An older Russian woman sat with them, saying in perfect English that she was there to "look after foreigners." She exchanged pleasantries about New York City, where she had worked in the 1920s as a strike organizer. This cautious atmosphere became more apparent at the kiddush reception presided over by the eighty-six-year-old Rabbi Lubanov and trusted synagogue leaders.

The white-haired scholar greeted us with a Bible lesson: "As the Jews had sinned twice during Isaiah's time they were given a double dose of punishment and subsequently a double amount of compassion. Therefore, since the Jews had suffered so greatly, I now look forward to the time when we *will get double compassion.*" We grasped his meaning.

Two days later, on the eve of Tish'a B'ov (day of mourning for the destruction of the First and Second Temples in Jerusalem—586 B.C.E. and 70 C.E.), we worshiped with congregants of the Kiev synagogue. As prayers filled the sanctuary, which had been without a rabbi since December 1961, we felt the great fear and hesitancy of communicating with foreigners. Officially, we were told: "We don't need your religious articles." Yet my last prayer book and prayer shawl were hungrily taken by two congregants. As he departed, Rabbi Hyman Schachtel of Houston felt someone taking the prayer book from his hand and whispering to him in Yiddish, "You have to be careful here. There are informers everywhere."

The Decline of Houses of Worship

Accounts of similar experiences are repeated by other visitors. The skeptic is likely to say: "How sad! But aren't these Jews victims of a general Soviet campaign against all religions?" Not so, according to Harrison Salisbury, who served as New York *Times* correspondent in Moscow for many years. "The Jewish religion has been a special target of the party drive. Synagogues have been closed, rabbis arrested, members of congregations intimidated and sometimes attacked. Especially in the Ukraine, a hotbed of anti-Semitism under the Tsars, there has been noted a revival of anti-Semitism, often encouraged by official party propaganda publications."[1]

Synagogues in the Soviet Union have declined in numbers from 1034 in 1917[2] to 60 today. They are at present served by three practicing rabbis and an unestimated handful of Hakhamin (scholars accepted as rabbis in oriental congregations). Some Soviet sources have placed the number of religious Jews as high as 500,000,[3] meaning that each congregation must serve more than 8000 people. This figure exceeds the membership in some of the most affluent synagogues in the West. (Temple Emanu-El of New York City, one of the world's largest congregations, has a membership of 2700 families.)

Even in the 1920s when the Yevsektsia waged a militant anti-religious campaign against rabbis and synagogues, there were still 934 synagogues in use.[4] Between 1956 and 1963 the authorities closed 354 of the 450 remaining synagogues.[5]

However, there exist some vestiges of a thriving Jewish religious life in some sections of the U.S.S.R. In Tbilisi, Georgia, where both an Ashkenazic and a Sephardic community function, Rabbi Miller addressed 1500 people at the synagogue. He said family units attended—grandfathers, fathers and children, functioning in accordance with full religious law. They operated a mikvah (ritual bath) and used three shochtim (ritual slaughterers).

Particularly during the Stalin purges, writers, editors and party functionaries produced a great deal of anti-Jewish propaganda aimed at discrediting those who attend the synagogues.

Lest one believe that their diatribes were merely a

part of the national atheistic campaign, the prominent British sovietologist and editor of *Jews in Eastern Europe*, Emanuel Litvinoff, reminds us that such literature appears today in greater volume and in more virulent and irrational tones than the apparent size of the religious movement warrants. He says it is clear that such books, pamphlets and articles are no more written for Jews than were *The Protocols of the Elders of Zion*. They were written to nourish the prejudices of existing anti-Semites and to engender hatred of Jews among those still free of it.[6]

Despite official denial of anti-Semitism, Soviet leaders have done little to alter the party line. Except for a bland editorial in *Pravda* on September 5, 1965, and a speech by Premier Alexei Kosygin at Riga, July 18, 1965, government officials have done little to follow Lenin's direction to educate the masses to understand that those who practice anti-Semitism harbor counterrevolutionary doctrines harmful to the state.

The Uzbek Outrages

As late as 1961, two days after Rosh Hashana (the Jewish New Year), in the U.S.S.R.'s Uzbek Republic in the city of Margelan, angry mobs sparked by tales of "blood ritual" (the ancient Christian canard had been recast for the Moslem faithful) assaulted, injured and looted Jewish victims. During one week, in this Central Asian community, authorities remained on the sidelines as Jews were attacked, homes broken into, furniture wrecked and personal possessions carried off. A year earlier, two other blood libel cases occurred, one in the Uzbek capital of Tashkent, and the other across the Caspian Sea, in Buinaksk, a town in the Daghestan Autonomous Republic.

On September 14, 1961, in Margelan, an inflamed group led by a man named Abdusatarov seized a Jewish woman, Mazol Yusupova, and charged her with kidnaping and killing Abdusatarov's two-year-old son by committing a ritual murder. They dragged her to the police where officials charged her with the crime. A local militia officer, Captain Akhmedov, accompanied by members of the mob, then ransacked Mrs. Yusupova's home, ostensibly looking for evidence. Similar searches were conducted in dozens of Jewish homes in the vicinity. The following morning the police arrested Dzhuru Israelov, Mrs. Yusupova's ninety-year-old father.

Omitting the blood-libel charges, news of the kidnaping received feature attention on local radio newscasts. Local mosques also broadcast the news. Rumors spread throughout the city that the woman had been arrested for murdering a Moslem child for Jewish ritual purposes. Angry mobs of Uzbek citizens roamed into the Jewish quarters unleashing their anger on the streets and homes. Clashes broke out as Jews defended themselves, since police authorities refused to heed pleas for protection. Riots lasted for six days until September 20, when guards set about restoring order in the city.

On October 7, the local paper, the Margelan *Khakikati*, reported a different version of the kidnaping. It seems the boy had been abducted by an Uzbek woman named Usmanova, residing in a nearby village, in her attempt to hide an abortion from her husband. Separated during her pregnancy and now reunited, the woman took Abdusatarov's child and brought him home to her husband as their own. Beyond these facts the newspaper reported nothing else. The riots and blood-libel rumors were left out of the story. Police participating in the riots received no punishment. Fear spread through the Jews of Margelan.

On May 9, 1962 in Tashkent, an Uzbek Moslem named Azizov led a group of ruffians as they broke into the home of Abigai Bangieva, a seventy-year-old shopkeeper. They charged the old woman with having taken blood from Azizov's young daughter for use in the Passover ritual. These accusations were sufficient for the authorities to order her arrest. The police imprisoned her and ransacked her home for evidence. Wild stories swept through the city: "Don't you know Jews use Moslem blood for religious purposes?" "All the Jews should be thrown out of the city!" Uncontrolled assaults followed on Jews, and panic spread through the Jewish community of 50,000.

Much later the facts came forth. On April 30, 1962, the young girl, after leaving Mrs. Bangieva's shop, had slipped and fallen, slightly cutting her ear. Azizov's Jewish hatred and uncontrolled imagination did the rest.[7]

In reporting these incidents to the West, B'nai B'rith president Label Katz, charged, "Neither the pogromists, local police or prosecutors have been punished or reprimanded. Omission of the facts in the Soviet press, and the silence of Soviet leaders can only provide local officials with encouragement to carry on similar actions."

Religious Targets

The penchant for propaganda, which by extension governs official conduct in such cases as the one above, also makes Jewish religious customs, holidays and ritual practices a favorite target in excerpts such as these:

THE SABBATH   Many believers in our country, unfortunately, continue to observe the Sabbath. They use various pretexts to absent themselves from work on this day, and so bring damage to the national economy. Many steps are of course being taken against these disrupters of labor discipline. Enlightenment work must nevertheless be stubbornly conducted among believers to show them all the impropriety of observing the Sabbath—a vestige of ancient savage rituals whose observance only debases the man of the socialist society.[8]

ROSH HASHANA and YOM KIPPUR (The New Year and Day of Atonement) The autumn holidays combined by the rabbis under the denomination of "Solemn Days," occupy a special place among the holy days of the Judean religion. These holy days can be traced back to the remote past, having resulted from a stratification of numerous magical rites established in different social-economic eras. They have absorbed the anti-scientific outlooks, rites, prayers, psalms and incantations, both of the primitive tribal system and of the slave-owning, feudal and capitalist class societies.

Stimulated by the mystical drug of the superiority of the Judean religion, and by the bourgeois-nationalistic propaganda on the national exclusivity of the Jewish people, these holy days aim to strengthen nationalistic feelings in the midst of believers.[9]

— As to the New Year, it is not mentioned in the Pentateuch at all. This ritual of hornblowing became *Rosh Hashana* only much later, in the period when an independent Jewish state existed. The *Yom Teruah* (the Day of the Blasting of the ram's horn—a synonym for the New Year) then acquired a new significance and purpose. Saadia Gaon, tenth-century Babylonian Jewish scholar and one of the most important Talmudists, explained the significance of the *Yom Teruah*—in other words, the *shofar* ritual of our own day, as follows: "On the New Year," he said, "the blowing of the horn must remind believers of Isaiah's prophecy of the future ingathering (in the Holy Land) of all the Jews scattered throughout the world."[10]

— The Kol Nidre prayer of Yom Kippur (Day of Judgment) is characteristic. Worshipers believe that on pronouncing this prayer, in which they beg God to release them from all promises, sins and oaths, they are literally relieved from all their obligations and transgressions. The prayer runs: "All promises, prohibitions, obligations and vows we have taken and sworn, or committed ourselves to, or pledged ourselves to, we repent on this day of all-forgiveness. May they be considered as sanctioned, forgiven, destroyed, non-existent and invalid. They will not bind us, nor have any force over us, promises will not be recognized as such, obligations as such, oaths as such."

This prayer not only educates believers in the spirit of deceit, but inculcates them with dishonesty toward other nations. "The right," which liberates Jews from oaths, incurs social-political damage. Fulfilling the commandments of this prayer, a Jewish believer can break military oaths, disclose state secrets, violate moral family obligations. He only has to read the prayer and he is absolved of his sins.[11]

SUCCOTH . . . a typical gay and festive holy day celebrated by the ancient cultivators on harvesting their corn and gathering their grapes. Nevertheless, this holiday carried a bright religious coloring. Having concluded their autumn work, farmers thanked and wooed the gods with all sorts of offerings. The holy day had a brightly expressed, magical character. Being powerless in their struggle for their crops, lacking knowledge in the laws and phenomena of nature, ancient Jews . . . expected to secure the restoration of nature's productive forces through magical, bewitching means. These rites belong partly to a series of customs for summoning the rain.

The Jewish religious autumn holy days are most harmful. Their danger lies in the fact that during the holy days ritual a nationalistic intoxication is kindled, and backward anti-scientific outlooks, whose origin can be traced to times of savagery and barbarism, are strongly preached. In capitalistic countries, in particular the U.S.A. and Israel, workers are inculcated with servile submission, meekness, humility, non-resistance to evil, and forgiveness of enemies. The "idea" of the unity of the Jewish nation, regardless of class affiliation, is widely propagated on holy days.[12]

PASSOVER . . . During the observance of holidays and customs, the rabbis orientate believers toward Jerusalem, as the spiritual center of the Judean religion. Even at present, Orthodox Jews celebrate Passover as a day of reunion with the Lord who will lead them to Israeli soil. This is symbolized in the traditional eating of Jerusalem matzo and the chanting of a psalm from the Torah: "God grant us to celebrate this day in Jerusalem, on Israeli soil, in the following year." It is no accident that almost yearly the Israeli rabbinate sends parcels of matzo to the Jewish synagogues in the Ukraine, including Lvov. However, don't the religious Jews know that Israel is

> at present an obedient tool in the hands of American, British and French imperialists?[13]

Actually, the traditional Passover prayer recalls the Jewish exile after the destruction of the Second Temple by the Romans (586 B.C.E.) and utters the hope that one day Jews would return to the Holy City. Until Theodor Herzl made this prayer a reality in the late 1800s, most Jews would have scoffed that such a prayer could become a reality. Reform Jews, even prior to Herzl, removed the prayer from their prayer books.

A favorite target of the propagandist is the "chosen People" concept. In an article called "Yahve Losing Supporters" printed in *Sovietskaya Moldavia* on July 7, 1966, M. Kogan writes:

. . . the teaching that of all the peoples of the earth, God chose, loved and raised high just the Jewish people, is one of the most harmful prejudices that the Jewish clergy are trying to impose on the believers. The reactionary dogma that the Jews are a chosen people is aimed, whether the adherents of Judaism want it or not, at erecting a sinister, blank wall between Jews and non-Jews and at preventing the fraternal unification of workers of all nationalities.

The Atheist's Concise Handbook (Korotky Dovidnik Ateista—1964) couples this theme with an attack on Zionism:

. . . Exploiting the religious dogma about the God-chosen people, modern Zionists wage reactionary propaganda about the exclusivity of the Jewish people, which, allegedly, is called to rule over all other peoples. They have unfolded a particularly unbridled propaganda and incite Jews against the other peoples that live in Palestine, kindle racial enmity and in every way support the imperialist policy of the ruling classes of Israel. It is the Zionists who were the inspirers of the Israeli aggression against Egypt. . . .

Attacks on the Bible and Rituals

Lest anyone believe that these writings are published in small quantities, one should look at the work of a Jewish atheist, Moishe Solomonovich Belenki, whose *What is the Talmud?*, published by the Soviet Academy of Sciences in an edition of 70,000 copies, attacks the ancient book as teaching reactionary ideas and exploiting morals. The author interprets the Talmud's disapproval of the *ignorance* of the man of the soil (similar to Lenin's slogan about the "idiocy of the village") as outright hostility to the man of the soil himself. Most non-Jewish scholars praise the Talmud. Jomo Kenyatta, president of Kenya, ordered a complete English-language version of the Talmud (which embodies 1000 years of Jewish history—c. 400 B.C.E.–500 C.E.) as a reference in redrafting Kenya's constitution.

Denigrating the Bible is the delight of the atheistic writer. The Bible's leading figures are portrayed as murderers, brutes, liars, degenerates, bloodthirsty aggressors, exploiters and money-mad profiteers, and the women as whores.

On Holy Scripture, Skepticism and Inquisition, by Antanas Petrika, describes King David as a "thief, liar, bandit, murderer and traitor." It claims that Abraham and Reuben were guilty of incest, and that Sarah was Abraham's sister as well as his wife. Three biblical heroines, Deborah, Yael and Esther, are depicted as lascivious, bloodthirsty and murderous.

The Prophets, however, are the real villains: "There never was another people whose priests knew so well how to exploit them as those of the ancient Jewish people." The author asserts that the Jews were never enslaved in ancient Egypt, but were rich and affluent there. According to him, they became so rich they remained there for 430 years.

This book is written in Lithuanian and was published in 1964 by the State Publishing House for Literature and Political Science, in Vilna. After they received numerous protests, authorities claimed that the remainder of the 7000 books printed were withdrawn from sale. Yet only two years later, Antanas Petrikas received a floral welcome at the Vilna airport. He was greeted by local literary, cultural and scientific luminaries and heralded by *Sovietskaya Litva* as the "well-known Lithuanian progressive in the U.S.S.R."

Regardless of a Jew's personal commitment to his faith, the religious customs basic to Judaism hold an important place for him. Even those unaffiliated with the synagogue will turn to the rabbi and the synagogue to ceremonialize a birth, a marriage or death, and very often to conduct a *bar mitzvah*. Even to Jews long divorced from the synagogue, and often members of the Communist Party, these traditions hold some meaning in their hearts. Therefore, Jewish ritual becomes another target.

Circumcision is characterized as "a softened form of ancient human sacrifices." The koshering of meat is equated with a lust for money, and the performance of koshering is said to be assigned "not to sanitary physicians, but people with medieval knowledge of medicine." Those who eat koshered meat are often stricken with brucellosis and other diseases, according to the propagandists.

The *bar mitzvah* ceremony is the life-wish of fanatical parents, who press upon their sons the study of basic Jewish tenets, thus distracting them from their studies in school. How cruel it is to be made to sweat over the dusty books of the ancient Bible when one can tread the bright paths of science. And as for the *mikvah* (ritual bath), the imputation is that because many people bathe there together, the water becomes laden with bacteria and the *mikvah* becomes a "nest of infection." The anti-Semitic author is almost visible in his repugnance of the "antiquated customs and ways of life that are alien to us."

So extreme are attacks on Jewish religious life in the Soviet Union that *Jewish Currents,* the leftist American monthly, stated in its July–August 1964 issue: "The persistence of non-historical primitive atheism in Soviet publications, which often seems to discredit the Jewish people, requires a thorough review by Soviet authorities."

Closing of Synagogues

Shutting down a synagogue is now routine for local authorities, who often convert the buildings into sports clubs, pioneer clubs, student apartments, warehouses and a variety of necessary state activities of greater priority than to "house the money-lenders and cheats of the God Jehovah." The authorities first usually coerce a group of synagogue members into signing a document confessing the evil deeds that are done within the sanctuary walls. In *Sovetskaya Moldavia,* August 5, 1960, for example, a statement appeared which had been sent to the newspaper by seven Jews. It read: "We consider that the time has come to tell all Jewish believers that the synagogue brings nothing to people but harm. We do not want to cheat workers and ourselves any longer and have consequently come to the conclusion that the existence of the synagogue serves no purpose." This, then, sets the stage for a grass-roots demand to accede to the citizens' request, which the newspaper supports with editorials and by printing letters to the editor.

Here, a few of many incidents:

In 1959, the Great Synagogue of Chernovtsy (Czernowitz), in the Ukraine, was closed on the charge that it was being used for "non-religious and illegal purposes" and housed "hooliganism and alcoholism," the latter referring to the sacramental use of wine. In the same year in Bobruysk, Byelorussia, a city of 100,000, of whom 60 per cent were Jewish, the synagogue also was closed, and Jews were threatened with arrest if private prayer meetings were held.

The synagogue at Tskhakaya, Georgia, had been sacked in 1962 at the height of the economic trials. The town's 2000 Jews raised funds to rebuild the structure and labored during autumn and winter to complete the task in time for Passover. A week prior to the service of dedication on the first Seder night, police officials told leaders of the congregation that the premises were required for other purposes. The doors were padlocked and the furniture removed.

In Minsk, in the midst of a prayer service in 1964, workmen began to remove the roof of the synagogue. Due to severe criticism from the West, authorities gave Jewish leaders permission to purchase a twenty-year-old, former private home, which would accommodate one hundred worshipers (the old synagogue seated thousands).

The action was termed unusual by the New York *Times*, since Minsk, whose 56,000 Jews constitute 9 per cent of the population, is on the main track of Western tourists ever curious about the country's churches and synagogues.

On November 5, 1962, news reached the West that the renowned synagogue of Lvov, the last remaining Jewish house of worship in the city, was forcibly shut down by Soviet authorities. Ritual objects, including a Torah inscribed by Emperor Franz Joseph of Austria, were confiscated. Local officials in co-operation with party organs took careful preparation to create an appearance to the general public that such closures were for the good of the proletariat and acted upon only after the irate demands of local citizens. Houses of worship, serving a total of 142,000 Jews, also were ordered closed that year in Sverdlovsk, Zhitomir, Kazan, Grozny, Zhmerinka, Belaya Tserkov, Kaunas, Kalarash and Piatigorsk.

Part of the groundwork for closing the Lvov synagogue was laid in an article of February 16, 1962, in *Lvov-*

skaya Pravda. In short-story form complete with dialogue, the piece describes a meeting in the synagogue between a money speculator and an elder. The furtive glances, haggling over the forbidden sale and purchase of gold coins, are described with penny-dreadful relish. The culprits are identified by name, and the alleged speculator is quoted as saying, "crooks and speculators of all types gather in the synagogue . . . and conclude all sorts of transactions there."

A member of the synagogue administration is trotted out as another exhibit, and this Jew willingly itemizes all manner of nefarious activities that take place in the building. The article is written in a way that could not deceive a ten-year-old Westerner, but apparently is accepted whole by many Russian adults.

Because of the visible taint upon the congregation, because of the hollow importunities of visiting Israeli diplomats, the congregation's leaders lose their prestige and authority, and many Orthodox Jews are "deeply angered by the spirit of profit and speculation which reigns in the 'holy abode.'"

The article takes pains not to castigate all Jews, but only the operators of a synagogue that "has become a place of criminal machinations which bring serious damage to our country and our people . . ." There follows the inevitable plea for public action—and thus another house of worship has been lost.

Paul Novick, editor of New York's leftist Yiddish daily, *Morning Freiheit,* challenged this Soviet action by asking: "If the synagogue is necessary because there are still those who like to have it and who need it, then why close it? Suppose the manager of a hotel were caught as a speculator, would that mean the hotel had to be shut?"[14]

Restrictions on Passover Matzos

Indications are that Soviet officials seem to have relaxed the restrictions on the baking of matzo for Passover. Today sufficient quantities seem available for the holiday observance. But until Western protests mounted, Kremlin authorities played a cat-and-mouse game with Russian Jews.

Playwright Arthur Miller once asked a Russian official, "Do you mean to tell me that the Soviet Union is endangered because a couple of Jews made a few matzos (unleavened bread) in a stove?" The official, it is said, blushed. However, the difficulties placed in the path of observant Jews by state authorities to prevent the baking of matzo essential to the observance of Passover merely serves as another device to intimidate Jews. Unlike some other holidays, Passover finds the committed and the uncommitted together at home. A Jewish guide of Intourist reluctantly confessed to me that although she did not believe in religion, out of respect for her parents she celebrated "the ceremony with them." Since the holiday recalls the Israelite exodus from Egypt under the leadership of Moses and the flight into the desert on the way to the Promised Land, Soviet leaders seem to prefer that such ancient recollections be forgotten.

Baking matzo in Russia requires either the use of state bakeries used by the synagogue or home facilities.

In 1957, Kharkov's 70,000 Jews were refused permits to produce the unleavened bread. Although the situation deteriorated, it was not until 1962 that Western circles received more accurate data on the new Soviet harassment. Most previous restrictions had been confined to cities off the tourist path (Lutsk, Stalino, Rostov, Saratov, Stalingrad, etc.). After the ban was applied to Odessa's Jews in 1959, and the following year to such tourist stops as Lvov, Chernovtsky and Kiev, Western circles could not have been surprised when, a few weeks prior to the Passover holiday in 1962, Rabbi Levin announced that Moscow's state baking facilities had broken down, and that despite promises of repairs, he finally had to urge his flock to eat peas as a substitute. The following year a new reason was provided for the absence of matzo: "It is unconstitutional and illegal for state bakeries to bake matzo and for state stores to sell them, because matzos are a religious article." The Soviet authorities had apparently changed policy at will, since a few years earlier, on July 11, 1956, an official document of the U.S.S.R. at the United Nations observed:

By order of the U.S.S.R. Government, on days preceding particularly important holidays—such as Passover in the case of Jews—the shops of the state trading organizations sell special types of bakery products, matzo for Orthodox Jews, etc., to enable worshipers to perform the appropriate ritual.

Anxious to defend these actions, Soviet propaganda machinery countered foreign criticism by stressing that a similar policy existed regarding the baking of kulichi (communion cakes), used during Easter by the Russian Orthodox Church. Although both are symbolic, matzo serves as an essential requirement for any Seder and must be eaten in place of bread and other leavened goods for the entire week of Passover. Moreover, the Church still produces sufficient symbolic kulichi in academy, monastery and seminary bakeries for use during the Easter holiday.

Early in 1963, permission was granted for Jews to bake matzo in their own homes and to receive gift parcels from abroad, undoubtedly due to foreign pressure. These practices were soon subjected to the usual official actions that tended to discourage them. In July 1963, four Jews were tried in Moscow and charged with selling matzo for profit. Subsequently, similar cases occurred and the Soviet press began printing attacks about Western matzo shipments and packages as "ideological sabotage" and "ideological subversion."

An article appeared in *Pravda Vostoka*, a newspaper of Tashkent in Uzbekistan, on March 17, 1964, calling upon Jews to return matzo parcels. The same story was printed five days later in *Izvestia*, giving official government credence and national notoriety to this unofficial policy. The following year, the New York *Times* of February 25, 1965, reported that the members of Moscow's two synagogues had received permission to bake matzo at rented facilities on the outskirts of the city. Rabbi Levin predicted that the plant set up by his congregation would produce 2200 pounds of matzo daily to supply his 10,000 congregants, with the surplus earmarked for the small Cherkizovo synagogue. The report added that, according to private Jewish sources, "Communal bakeries have also been set up in Leningrad, and perhaps in Kiev, but in other parts of the Soviet Union, Jewish communities had not received permission." These sources also urged Jews in the United States and Western Europe not to abandon their efforts to ship matzo to Jewish communities in the Soviet Union, and thought the improvement in Moscow and Leningrad was primarily the result of the publicity the last year's shortage had received abroad.

One month before Passover 1965, Label Katz, president of B'nai B'rith, reported the news that Soviet officials had banned the baking of matzo in the entire Ukraine, where some 37 per cent of all Soviet Jews live. He considered the availability of matzo in Leningrad and Moscow a technique "to satisfy foreign journalists and visitors" and added that purchasers of matzo "were paying between 75 and 85 cents a pound in Moscow, as compared to between 35 and 45 cents in New York City. This in itself is, in the Soviet context, an inhibiting factor . . . since incomes and standards of living are far lower than those in our own country." Also, most of the synagogue congregants are pensioners.

The Innocent Messengers

Western visitors are frequently used as innocent messengers to bear tidings of Soviet promises for future improvement in the religious or cultural conditions of the Jewish community. At the Ministry of Cults it was volunteered to us that 5000 new prayer books would appear by the end of July 1966, and another 5000 would be ready a month later. In addition, during the month of September, religious calendars would be made available and an abundance of matzo the following spring. Rabbi Levin's story to our group varied slightly: There could be prayer books, since the plates were ready; however, permission for the paper had not been received. Apparently, an acute paper shortage hit the country at this time, since the Baptists told us of a similar "no paper" ploy regarding their new hymnals.

The previous year, Rabbi Miller and his delegation from the Rabbinical Council of America had been assured by their Moscow colleagues that 10,000 new prayer books were expected shortly. At the same time, Aaron Vergelis, editor of the Yiddish weekly *Sovietish Heimland,* and a leading Soviet apologist on Jewish matters, who was then visiting Argentina, told the Jewish press there that the prayer books had already been printed on his magazine's presses and were ready for distribution. Rabbi Arthur Schneier, president of the Appeal of Conscience Foundation, learned during his 1966 visit to the Soviet Union that Rabbi Levin had explained to the authorities that because Yiddish letters lacked vowels they could not be used as type face for a Hebrew prayer book. However, a year later, in April 1967, Rabbi Schneier found "definite progress." Rabbi Levin had been summoned to a printing factory where the foreman showed the rabbi some old, dusty plates in a Hebrew type face that turned out to be the same used for the limited edition of 3000 prayer books published in 1956. Fifty of the 430 plates were damaged and Rabbi Schneier said that during his visit he saw the damaged plates replaced with new ones and made ready for production.

"We were told," Rabbi Schneier said, "that after the

allocation of paper and the assignment of a printing plant, the prayer books would soon be finished." The next excuse given to various inquiring critics was that the paper would be needed to glorify the Fiftieth Anniversary celebrations of the October Revolution.

The Russians must have run out of excuses. As Rabbi Levin departed for his American tour in June of 1968, he carried a suitcase full of new prayer books as souvenirs to America. At the same time Novosti, the Soviet news agency, announced that 10,000 new siddurs had been published. The volume contained the basic prayers for Jewish festivals and other occasions and included the phrase uttered at the conclusion of the service on the Day of Atonement and at the end of the Passover Seder ritual—"Next year in Jerusalem." This statement is a favorite weapon of the propagandist in seeking to prove a Russian Jew's disloyalty to the motherland.

Were the prayer books actually published or just produced in limited numbers for exploitation? Returning visitors report that the book, priced at two rubles, could be purchased in Moscow for prices ranging from eleven to thirteen rubles. Leaders of the synagogue in Moscow and Odessa will show off the new book, but in Leningrad there are no copies. Worshipers in Moscow, Leningrad and other congregations also must still be content with the use of their worn and threadbare prayer books.

The Russian Orthodox Church

Although not so potent a political force as it was during Tsarist times, the Orthodox Church is still the most influential and cohesive non-Communist movement in Soviet Russia.[15]

Communist officials wonder how, after great barrages of anti-religious propaganda, most churches still manage to survive under the political system. True, they have adapted to the prescribed codes and modified their theistic doctrines to conform with Marxist-Leninist ideology, yet fifty years of atheist education in schools, and persistent, sometimes brutal, pressure against churches and their members have not yielded the results the Communist Party expected. Religion has not died. To the contrary, if we can believe the National Council of Churches publication, *Religion in Communist Dominated Areas*, there were indications in 1967 that "religious belief and the longing for mystical experience sprang up in 1967 among youths and intellectuals, perhaps more significantly than among their 1917 predecessors."[16]

The periodical's editor, Paul B. Anderson, told me in an interview that within the past five years, various branches of the Soviet Academy of Science conducted sociological and religious surveys to determine the extent of church attendance among Soviet youth. They found that the percentage of young people participating in church services had been reduced, but nevertheless still continued. Dr. Anderson, a leading authority on Christianity in the Soviet Union, pointed out that usually the youth who aims at a university education is reluctant to identify with the church. "When you get beyond high school, any relationship with religion is precluded and frowned upon. Any youngsters found openly engaged in church activities would find difficulty in entering a university." However, he added that many who are part of the agricultural and working classes do not go to college, and these people do relate to the church. Especially, Anderson noted, this applies to girls. The boys tend to shy away since they are anxious to get ahead in their professional activity and do not want local officials holding such participation against them. Even so, 40 to 50 per cent of married people affiliated with the church still baptize their children.

Soviet officials concerned about this religious ferment have alerted regional delegates of the State Council on Religion Affairs to provide them with lists of people baptized or married in a church ceremony. Such "deviates" are then inundated with atheistic material to swing them back to the party line. Undoubtedly, many party officials were embarrassed when the U.S.S.R.'s most prominent defector in recent years, Joseph Stalin's daughter, Svetlana Alliluyeva, admitted she had been baptized as recently as May 1962, by a Russian Orthodox priest. Furthermore, she admitted a belief in God: "For me, God is just the power of life and justice, and when I am talking about God I am just talking about happiness to live and to enjoy life on this earth."[17]

Of course, Christian baptism does not leave a religious identification such as the comparable Jewish and Moslem ceremony of circumcision, although circumcision is a common medical practice in the United States and other Western countries. Rabbi Miller found that excepting in Georgia and a few other republics that have large Moslem populations, Jews cannot be circumcised anywhere in the Soviet Union, particularly since there are no "mohels" (professional practitioners of circumcision).

Despite limitations under the Communist system, the strength of the Orthodox Church prevails. Recently, Metropolitan Nikodim presided over an "extremely useful" dialogue between Russian Orthodox leaders and Western Catholics. The theological discussions were aimed at improving relations between the two Christian bodies. When one of the Orthodox Russian priests was asked how his church fared in the U.S.S.R. compared to Jews and other religious groups, he answered: "You cannot place us in the same category as other religious groups in the Soviet Union. We are in our own homes. We are not strangers or guests."

Comparative statistics between church and synagogue activities demonstrate the difference dramatically. Last available information in 1961 showed 20,000 parishes and 22,000 priests. This figure, according to officials at the World Council of Churches has been reduced in both categories to about 6000 and 8000. The 1969 annual calendar or almanac, bearing a color cover, presented seventy-five photographs of the bishops in the Church. In addition to the annual yearbook, the Orthodox Church publishes a monthly eighty-page journal (*Zhurnal Moskovsky Patriarkhii*), and manufactures crucifixes, icons and candles. The annual estimated income in Moscow alone amounts to six million rubles from the sale of eighteen million candles. Orthodox prelates attend regular international congresses and maintain membership in the World Council of Churches.

Church seminaries have been reduced from eight in

1960 to three today in Leningrad, Moscow and Odessa. The same buildings and faculties in Moscow and Leningrad conduct academies teaching graduate studies. When we visited Moscow, Bishop Feloret told us that "we are getting three times as many applicants for the theological schools as needed." By contrast, Rabbi Levin bemoaned his inability to recruit any young men for the rabbinate. A dingy classroom in the Moscow Central Synagogue has been put aside as a Yeshiva (theological school). But there are no dormitories, and housing permits for out-of-town students must be obtained from, and at the discretion of, local officials. At the end of 1963, only five students remained at the school because authorities had turned down the applications for residential permits from eight young Georgian and Central Asian Jews.[18]

Funds allocated by Moscow's Jews for a new Yeshiva were also rejected by the authorities and designated, instead, for use as a repair fund for a wing in the synagogue. Rabbi Miller's delegation learned from Rabbi Levin that twenty housing permits would be granted by local officials. A year later, this story was changed when the rabbi told us, "We can have all the students we want, but our young men are only interested in secular subjects and science."

The Status of Other Religions

As another contrasting example, the twenty-five million Moslems of the Soviet Union published a new edition of the Koran in 1963. They also send pilgrims to

Mecca and Medina. When Dr. Anderson visited their seminary in 1961 at Bokhara, Uzbekistan, he found forty young men training as imams (Moslem ministers). Moslem students are permitted to enroll in theological academies, in Cairo, Damascus and Morocco, while Jewish students are not even permitted to study at the excellent, though small, seminary in Budapest. In 1969 a visiting American Orthodox rabbi received word from the Ministry of Religion that one student would soon begin his rabbinic studies in Budapest, a fact as yet unconfirmed.

The Baptists, the most dynamic body of believers in the Soviet Union today, flourish within the framework of state dogma. The All-Union Council of Evangelical Christian Baptists directs the 5000 churches and three million adherents. Their leaders told us they were only allowed to train ministers through correspondence courses, but showed us copies of Bibles, hymnals, prayer books and a bimonthly publication, *Bratskii Vestnik* (Fraternal Herald). The Baptist service we attended in Moscow featured a vigorous choir of 120 middle-aged people singing for the overflowing worshipers, most of whom were older people. The Baptists claimed young people attended the later service and said a young choir sang at the services three times a week. The Baptists communicate with, and visit, member churches, conduct liturgical and musical conferences and hold regional church conclaves.

Most of the country's Catholics, who live in Latvia and Lithuania, benefited from the Vatican's friendly attitude with Moscow. After the Ecumenical Council, which had been attended by Russian Orthodox observers, conditions improved somewhat with the appointment of a new bishop in each republic, the reduction of atheistic propaganda, and a new limited flow of liturgical material.

Despite the country's increasing campaign against religion, the church manages to survive under the pressure of party propaganda. Religion (in curtailed form) still shows life after more than fifty years of Communist rule. Only the Jews who cling to the synagogue—as a class— seem destined for oblivion.

V
Jews as Second-class Citizens

Despite constant attempts by the Kremlin toward greater Russification, adherence to nationality is part of a Soviet citizen's daily existence. Westerners, especially Americans, find it difficult to accept the nationality concept since in the United States one's ethnic heritage, although remembered, plays a subordinate role to that of being an American.

Except for Jews, whose way of life is classified as a nationality, the U.S.S.R.'s 108 other nationalities speak their various languages without hindrance, attend their ethnic schools and enjoy their ancient cultures.

The Dangerous Identity Card

Soviet nationality rights were guaranteed by the Constitution of 1918 and by further articles in the Republics. Almost from the beginning, however, there was a question whether Jews qualified for the same consideration. The Lenin-Stalin categorization of Jews classified them as second-class citizens, and the internal-passport system perpetuates this.

Under a law enacted in 1932 (originally initiated as a means of allotting housing facilities during the great influx to the cities) all Soviet citizens must carry nationality identity cards upon reaching the age of sixteen. This exposes the Jew to officials and government agencies when he applies for a job, for admission to an educational institution or when seeking new housing. "The Soviet Jew thus gets the worst of both worlds," commented Leonard Schapiro, professor of political science at London University, and a specialist in Soviet Government and politics. "He is not allowed to forget that he is not quite a Russian, and he is not allowed to develop as a member of a separate national community with its own culture, its own religion and its own tradition."[1]

The Cultural Desert

Ever since the Stalin purges, Jews have existed in a cultural desert. After 1948, their institutions were abolished on the ground that Jews were linguistically assimilated, a party line still adhered to. There were 2,268,000 Jews in the Soviet Union according to the 1959 census, although even Soviet sources believe the figure to be more than three million.[2] Jews rank eleventh in population. The census also showed that 487,786 Jews or 18 per cent, considered Yiddish or Yiddish dialects to be their native tongue, a sharp decline from the figure of 70 per cent in the 1927 census. In an analysis published by the Warsaw Historical Institute, the publication felt that "native language" was undefined in the 1959 Soviet census. As a result, the survey believed many who spoke and read Yiddish and who appreciated Yiddish culture, never-

theless gave Russian as their language since they spoke it
at work and in the street, and to an extent, at home.[3]
One must also take into account the lingering fear among
Jews, because of the years under Stalin, that makes them
reluctant to identify their "Jewishness" to the authorities
unless absolutely necessary.

Discrimination against Jewish culture, especially when
compared with other nationalities, reaches alarming pro-
portions. Neither Yiddish nor Hebrew are among the
fifty-nine languages of instruction in Soviet schools. There
are no Yiddish daily newspapers other than the *Birobidzhaner Stern* (circulation 1000), described by Rabbi
Ely E. Pilchik of Newark during our trip as, "The type
is Yiddish; the content, Russian."

During the ten-year period, from 1949 to 1958, no
Yiddish books were published in the Soviet Union. From
1959–66, thirteen titles were printed, for an estimated
total of 210,500 books. The once-great Yiddish theater
has diminished to a few amateur groups, such as the
one in Vilna, and some aging professionals and concert
artists who play to overflow audiences.

Sovietish Heimland

Only one magazine in Yiddish exists, the monthly
Sovietish Heimland, which is under the supervision of
Aaron Vergelis, a party-oriented editor. The publication
has a reported circulation of 25,000 copies and is distributed in the West to pacify critics of Soviet infringe-
ment upon the cultural rights of Jews.

"We're keepers of the culture," a group of editors told

us in the editorial offices in Moscow. Launched as a
bimonthly in August 1961, after a thirteen-year absence
of all Jewish publications, the magazine became a
monthly in January 1965. The editors claim that 120 to
130 Yiddish writers work on the 160-page publication.
"Some are editors, some are poets, some are literary and
artistic critics," we were informed. The spokesman, a Mr.
Muni Schulman, stressed his Communist Party membership and firm commitment to atheism, although, he said
apologetically, "We have no quarrel with those who believe in God."

Vergelis (who was not at our meeting), during his
1963 visit to the U.S.A., told a New York *Herald Tribune* reporter: "They threw me out of the Communist
Party. I even lost my membership in the Writer's Union
of the U.S.S.R. I believed in Stalin as one believes in
God."[4] During his visit here he was boycotted by all
national Jewish organizations. The Synagogue Council
of America urged American Jewry not to be beguiled
by one of the architects of Judaism's destruction in the
Soviet Union. Others described him as a party hack,
and one "whose cordial relationship with the Soviet security police was a half-open secret."[5]

Some authorities consider that projects like *Sovietish
Heimland* require encouragement rather than criticism.
They recognize that the assimilation process plagues both
Western and Soviet Jews, but remind us we must never
forget that the isolated Russian Jew cannot channel his
identity through religious affiliation or in social and cultural activities, as do his brethren in other countries. The
use and preservation of Yiddish remain the only means

by which the individual and the community can assert their Jewishness, as they did in the past. Jacob Sonntag, editor of the *Jewish Quarterly* in Great Britain, is of the opinion that "We should realize that here, as elsewhere, the remnants of Yiddish cultural tradition are engaged in a hard struggle to maintain, and to continue in that tradition. It is not just the language—it is a way of life, a set of values, an attitude to people and society."[6]

Such token concessions as *Sovietish Heimland,* and the books permitted to be printed, lend credence to the remark made in 1961 by Yekaterina Furtseva, the present Minister of Culture, to André Blumel, vice-chairman of the France-Soviet Friendship Society, that if the U.S.S.R. "did anything at all (for Yiddish culture), it would not be for domestic reasons, but to please our friends abroad."[7]

Reactions from the West

The 1948 eradication of Jewish cultural institutions by Stalin brought numerous queries from the West. Especially curious were leftist Socialists and Communists—strong advocates of Yiddish—anxious to know why such a rich reservoir of creativity had been wiped out.

One such query came from J. B. Salsberg, a member of the Canadian Parliament and of Canada's Communist Party. In 1956 he spent some time in the Soviet Union meeting with officials, including former Premier Khrushchev, only to be told that "integration (Russification) caused the cessation of Jewish cultural activities." Mr.

Salsberg did not accept this explanation and told the Soviet leaders, "At this very moment there are very large numbers of Soviet Jews who desire and need, even crave, Jewish cultural and communal expression."[8]

Soviet officials are frequently caught in their own propaganda. Two years after the Salsberg visit, Danilov, the U.S.S.R.'s Deputy Minister of Culture, told a delegation of Jewish French Communists that "Last year (1957), three million Jews attended three thousand Yiddish concerts."

"If there is such an interest, would not similar demands be found for other cultural activities?" the visitors asked. Danilov replied, "We realize this is an important matter. It is undergoing a process of development and it must be pondered. It has to be solved and we must assume a respectful attitude."

Danilov's parting words to the delegation were: "You know very well the difficulties of the past. Today, this matter is in the process of full development. A little time is still needed and everything will be normalized: All will be well again."[9]

In his report, Dr. Hayim Sloves, a Yiddish journalist and a member of the French delegation, called upon fellow Communists to "condemn categorically and publicly" the crimes of Stalin's Black Years and to "expose the false theoretical presumptions, which serve to justify this tragedy. . . . A progressive Jewish culture cannot develop if we accept the canard that Jewish national peculiarity in deed and word, as well as script, is a stumbling block, a hindrance on the road to Socialism, and that only integration means progress."[10]

Sholom Aleichem

Even Sholom Aleichem, the most widely read Jewish author from Russia, has fallen victim to assimilation. In 1949, after mounting pressure from the outside, the Soviet Committee for World Peace altered its original plan to omit Sholom Aleichem from the roster of those to be honored.

In a record sixteen days, Soviet publishers produced a volume of the author's short stories. The 30,000 copies were quickly sold. Moscow theaters were filled during concert readings and dramatic presentations of the author's work, and as a grand tribute, a commemorative postage stamp was issued.

B. Z. Goldberg, distinguished Yiddish writer and Sholom Aleichem's son-in-law, estimates that since the revolution ten to twelve million volumes of his father-in-law's books were sold in the Soviet Union, most of these in other than the Yiddish language. In May 1966, a nationwide tribute honored the fiftieth anniversary of his death. Today, however, a visitor passing Sholom Aleichem's final residence at 5 Red Army Street in Kiev can see the white marble plaque with the inscription, "A great writer . . ." altered during the time of Stalin from "The Great Jewish writer . . ."

The Need for Cultural Restoration

Many Jews outside the Soviet Union cannot grasp the need for constant emphasis on the restoration of Yiddish culture for Soviet Jews. According to B. Z. Goldberg, "It is wrong to look at the Russian situation from the vantage point of a Western Jew. American Jews mistakenly equate the question of Yiddish in the U.S.S.R. with Yiddish on the American scene. They say, 'Well, people don't speak Yiddish here, either. There are few people buying Yiddish books and there exists no Yiddish publishing house in the States.' An American Jew does not require a knowledge of Yiddish or Hebrew to become familiar with the history, heritage and customs of his people, because there is a vast amount of material printed in English. There is nothing comparable in the Russian language. Even the literature available prior to the revolution has been placed in museums and libraries where no one but trusted intellectuals and scholars can touch it."

The Russians are quick to announce the appearance of any Jewish cultural items. Early in 1965, a Yiddish book, *Azoy Leben Mir*, was published, consisting of twenty articles, most of which had been published in *Sovietish Heimland*. Eighteen articles dealt with the prosperity and well-being of the Soviet Jew. Another article depicted the "impoverished" Jewish life in America. The final contribution was sixty pages long, glorifying Jewish life in Birobidzhan where less than 10 per cent of the population is Jewish.

Emanuel Litvinov, editor of the British quarterly, *Jews in Eastern Europe*, declared: "The book represents Jews in an advanced stage of assimilation. They are soldiers, scientists, electricians, engineers, collective farmers and so on. Indistinguishable from non-Jews, except for an occasional partiality to traditional Jewish food. None of the essays indicates that there are Jews who speak Yiddish, nor are there references to Jewish culture or religious Jews. The intention of the book is plainly propagandist and, therefore, valueless to Jews who live in the U.S.S.R."[11]

Nevertheless, the Russians were anxious for the West to know about the book. Both Tass and Novosti news agencies announced its appearance and availability in Moscow bookstores. Novosti stated that 15,000 copies had been published, with 5000 distributed to the Russian Federation Trade network, 3000 sent to the Ukraine, more than 1000 to Leningrad, and more than 3000 to Minsk. "The book," Novosti reported, "aroused a great interest among Jewish readers. For instance, the bookshop in Kirov Street, in the center of Moscow, sold one hundred copies in an hour." Yet, on January 31, 1965, a New York *Herald Tribune* correspondent reported that when he sought the book at several stores he was told in one that eighty copies had been received and sold, and in another, that the store was closing to take inventory. Inquiries for the book were also made without avail by correspondents of the British Broadcasting Corporation's Moscow bureau. They finally located copies at *Sovietish Heimland*.

If adequate numbers of Yiddish newspapers were published, they too would find a similar enthusiastic readership. Dr. Sloves reported seeing long lines of people at Moscow's Lenin Library waiting to register weeks in advance to read Yiddish newspapers from foreign countries. He said, "These papers have been so widely read and passed through so many eager hands, they are almost unreadable." The journalist was amazed to see youngsters reading the papers, trying to learn Yiddish.[12]

Statistics prepared from Soviet sources show startling comparisons between cultural facilities granted Jews and those permitted other Soviet nationalities. (See chart below.) The Yakuts, a Mongoloid people of eastern Siberia, published twenty-seven newspapers in 1966 to serve a total population of 236,655. This Turkic-speaking nationality practicing shamanism, a faith that holds to the supernatural powers of shamans, or medicine men, produced in the same year 119 belles-lettres publications, and books in a quantity of 1,388,000. In 1966, four books, or 26,000 volumes in Yiddish, were allowed the Jews. The following table depicts some cultural comparisons in 1966:[13,14]

The Soviet Government continues to answer critics with the official line that "Jews are not a proper nationality, have no territory of their own, and there is no reason why they should have separate cultural institutions, or publications," etc.[15] The argument is hollow when one compares the treatment accorded the dispersed Germans who rank thirteenth in number—1,619,655—while Jews rank eleventh.

The Germans in Russia

The existence of the Germans in Russia dates back to 1550. Their numbers increased greatly during the Westernization programs of Catherine the Great (1762–96) and Alexander I (1801–25). At the time of World

Nationality	Population Total	Periodicals and Annual Circ.	Newspapers	Belles-Lettres Publications	Books
JEWS	2,267,814	1 (192,000)	1	no data	4 (26,000)
UDMURTS	624,794	3 (90,000)	18	13 (282,000)	23 (95,000)
MARIS	504,205	3 (90,000)	13	39 (282,000)	78 (274,000)
KOMIS KOMPERMIAKS	430,928	2 (76,000)	4	13 (336,000)	22 (93,000)
YAKUTS	236,655	2 (190,000)	27	34 (810,000)	85 (578,000)
BASHKIRS	989,040	13 (1,349,000)	22	66 (1,427,000)	135 (792,000)

War I, laws were enacted to confiscate German property, close down newspapers and ban the German language. German schools were Russified, and some 200,000 Germans were deported to Siberia. The Bolshevik government eventually restored their rights, and in 1924 the Volga German Autonomous Soviet Socialist Republic was founded, although German ethnic institutions still were banned.

During the Stalin purges Germans suffered the fate imposed upon others, and after the Nazi invasion of Russia, large numbers were deported to the Komi Autonomous Soviet Socialist Republic and Central Asia. The status of the German remained unchanged until 1954 when Konrad Adenauer, while on a visit to Moscow to negotiate diplomatic relations, requested "as a humanitarian matter . . . the repatriation of German prisoners of war and other German citizens still held by the Soviets."

Influenced by this appeal, the Supreme Soviet on December 13, 1955, ordered the release of Germans from special settlements and forced-labor camps and ordered the end of their surveillance by the secret police.[16] Full restoration of rights was granted by a decree of the Soviet Presidium, dated August 29, 1964, which deplored injustices carried out against Germans, praised them for their role in the victory over the Nazis, and commended them for playing "an active part" in the postwar Communist society.

For the Germans, such a decree meant complete exoneration, with full and equal rights, and the promise of co-operation by the government for establishment of all desired facilities, although their former territory along the Volga River was not restored.

Similar exoneration was granted the 500,000 Crimean Tatars in September 1967. Charged with being Nazi collaborators, the Tatars had been banished from their former republic in the Crimea, now a part of the Ukraine, to their present homes in the Uzbek, Kazakh and Tadzhik republics. Like the Germans, they were not allowed to return to their former republic, but local Central Asian authorities have been ordered to "assist and co-operate" in providing for the Tatar nationality a full economic and cultural life in accordance with Tatar national interests and traits. The rehabilitation decree criticizes past accusations against the Tatars, stating that only a certain segment of the people collaborated with the Nazis, and therefore the nationality group as a whole should not have been condemned.[17]

It did not take long for the mandate rehabilitating the Germans to open the cultural floodgates. Eleven days after the law was adopted, the Central Radio Council of Kazakhstan gave permission for its German-language broadcasts to be picked up by other stations throughout the nation and held for delayed programing, if necessary. These offered German-language instruction, discussions about facets of Communist political activity, music and other cultural features. Today, radio and television shows in German are produced all over the country, and Radio Moscow beams two broadcasts daily abroad.

The last available figures, issued in 1964 (prior to the exoneration decree, it should be noted), show that 13,-015,000 copies of 223 books were published. Thirty-five books were written by East German authors, fourteen by West Germans, and eighty-nine were translations into German. Large numbers of books also were imported from both East and West Germany. Recently, the editor of the Progress Publishing House, Moscow, responsible for foreign-language publications, pledged to produce "every second day—a new book (in German)."

Several German-language newspapers exist today, which are published in Moscow, Slavgorod and other areas. A weekly newspaper, *Neues Leben* (New Life), a sixteen-page tabloid, is published by *Pravda* as the "official organ of the German population." It regularly reports on a wide range of news and cultural activities.

German parents may send their children either to ethnic schools covering grades one through eleven, where courses are taught exclusively in their national language, or to "regular" schools using Russian, where mother-tongue instruction is available in grades two through eight. Where an adequate German curriculum is not offered, parents complain vehemently. *Neues Leben* prints letters of protest, offers editorial support and directs complaints against local officials to appropriate educational authorities.

There are also special departments for training German schoolteachers; pedagogic classes are held in German in certain secondary schools, and a large number of textbooks are written and published in German.

The Lack of Educational Facilities

In contrast, there are no classes of any kind for Jews, either in Yiddish, Hebrew or Russian, anywhere in the nation. Jewish youngsters, therefore, are hard put to learn about their past or customs. Soviet officials often postulate: "We'd give Jews classes, but no one makes any request for such instruction."

Although in 1961, the Twenty-second Party Congress guaranteed "complete freedom for each citizen of the U.S.S.R. to speak, rear and educate his children in any language,"[18] a mere two years earlier, Vyachleslav P. Yelyutin, Minister of Higher and Secondary Education, while on a tour of the United States, on September 29, 1959, told a reporter: "There will be no revival of Yiddish-language schools." He offered as an excuse that Jews were scattered among other nationalities, and that if they did learn Yiddish, "They would not be able to work effectively with their non-Jewish fellow citizens." The Russian Soviet Federal Socialist Republic, which most people mean when they refer to "Russia," has a Jewish population of one million, but no classes of any type for Jews, as such. Two minority groups in the republic—the Chukchi with 12,000 people and the Koryaks with 6300— are, on the other hand, given adequate educational facilities.

In the Ukraine, where there also are one million Jews, the historically ostracized Polish minority of 363,000 has three "nationality" schools; the 239,000 Moldavians have 157 schools, and the 149,000 Hungarians, 99 schools.

According to Minister Yelyutin's claim, a resounding 10 per cent of students in colleges and universities are Jewish, and there is no quota system![19] In a letter to the New York *Times* published September 29, 1969, Solomon Schwarz termed Yelyutin's statement "patently wrong." He cited 1957 figures of the Central Statistical Adminis-

tration, in the Russian Soviet Federated Socialist Republic, as listing a total of 1,266,700 students, and that the
following years the same body showed that 51,563 students in that republic were Jewish.

"Even if we were to suppose," Schwarz said, "that in
the other fourteen Soviet republics together, the percentage of Jews in institutions of higher education was slightly
higher . . . the number of Jews among the students of
all Soviet institutions of higher education could reach
only little more than 4 per cent."

In a study of Soviet education practices, in May 1964,
Professor Nicholas De Witt of Indiana University found
that 3.22 per cent of the student population in Soviet universities was Jewish. Dr. De Witt stated that a nationality quota system based on a "policy directive"
exists. "If the share of Jewish applicants is high, the
admissions are cut back and preferences are given to
other nationals. Access of Jews to higher education is
far below the proportionate representation of Jews in
the urban population of Byelorussia, Uzbekistan, Georgia, Lithuania and Moldavia."

Despite a higher percentage of Jewish urbanization,
and of Jews speaking Russian instead of Yiddish, "official government statistics demonstrate clearly," he said,
"that Soviet authorities are employing a quota system to
reduce the proportion of Jews enjoying opportunities of
higher education. While Soviet Jews still attend universities in the U.S.S.R. in a proportion exceeding their
statistical representation in the country at large, the evidence shows that this proportion is steadily and rapidly
decreasing."[20]

Soviet Response; Jewish Rebuttal

Whenever Soviet authorities respond to criticism, a nerve has been tapped. One such response was made to columns written by B. Z. Goldberg in November 1966, in the Yiddish daily, *Der Tag*, and the Israeli newspaper, *Al Hamishmar*. Grigory Osipov, an editor of Novosti and a craftsman of virulent anti-Semitism, challenged Goldberg's remarks about university restrictions. Osipov cited 1966–67 admissions at Lomonosov University in the department of natural sciences, where 2251 students were accepted. Of these, 1804 were Russians, 233 Jews, 114 Ukrainians, 40 Byelorussians, 21 Tatars, 18 Armenians, 13 Uzbeks and 8 Georgians. In the humanities department, of a total 1100 students, 933 were Russians, 62 Ukrainians, 55 Jews, 12 Byelorussians, 11 Kazakhs, 9 Armenians, 9 Tatars and 9 Uzbeks. The Novosti editor supplied figures for the same year from the State University in Odessa, where, out of 110 students accepted for day classes in the department of physics, 51 were Russians, 40 Ukrainians, 16 Jews and 3 represented other nationalities; in evening courses there were 24 Russians, 16 Ukrainians, 8 Jews and 2 others.

Goldberg viewed the Soviet figures as "suffering from errors." He said that although Soviet Jews comprised 1.1 per cent of the total population, most of them were concentrated in urban areas where they made up 10 to 25 per cent of the residents. Unless Jews are restricted, he said, they traditionally provide a higher percentage of students. According to him, the Jewish population of

Odessa is more than 20 per cent. Of the Moscow University figures, Goldberg wonders whether the statistics showing Jewish students comprising 10 per cent in the sciences and only half that in the humanities means that when good scientists are wanted, the abilities of the applicants are given greater consideration. Finally, Goldberg rejected the comparison of a Russian Jewish population of 1.1 per cent to 3 per cent of Jews among college students with the reminder that prior to World War II, Jews comprised 13 per cent of the total student body.[21]

In the United States, during the height of quota clauses in the 1920s and 1930s, actual discriminatory practices were difficult to document. In the Soviet Union, such information becomes nearly impossible to obtain. Mrs. Svetlana Alliluyeva, the daughter of Stalin, responded to a question during a television interview in the United States that she, personally, had encountered discrimination in education against Jews. "I know about restrictions in universities and in the institutes when very talented Jewish people are not admitted, and instead, people of other nationalities who are less talented are enrolled."[22]

Jews are conspicuously scarce in the military, in higher echelons of the government and in the diplomatic service of the Soviet Union. Soviet statistics, however, repeatedly cite high percentages of Jews in the arts, sciences and medicine, and claim 10.4 per cent of the nation's prosecutors, judges and lawyers to be Jews.

In a report before the House Foreign Affairs Committee on May 11, 1965, Dr. Joseph B. Schectman, author and Soviet expert, said, "Jews are strikingly underrepresented in the legislative bodies of the Soviet Union, and their representation is steadily shrinking." A report by the London *Jewish Chronicle* announced the election of the same five Jewish members to the Supreme Soviet of the U.S.S.R. in June 1966. The publication said, "The proportional percentage fell . . . because the Chamber of Nationalities was enlarged by 98 deputies. Both chambers have 72 more deputies than the previous Supreme Soviet. Jews make up less than 3 per cent of the 1517 deputies, far below the nationality ratio of Jews in the total Soviet population, thus making Jews . . . heavily underrepresented in the Supreme Soviet."

The elected members were: Binyamin Emmanvilovich Dymshyts, a deputy prime minister, and therefore the most prominent Jew in the government; Yuli Borisovich Khariton, academician; Rafael Chaimovich Khersonsky, a turner in a factory; Alexander Borisovich Chakovsky, a writer and secretary of the executive of the Writers' Union, and the late Illya Grigorievich Ehrenburg. The last three were elected to the Chamber of Nationalities.

The *Jewish Chronicle* states that "Except for Kheronsky, delegate for a district of Birobidzhan, all the Jewish deputies were elected by districts lacking Jewish consciousness. Chakovsky, by replacing a Jewish army general, Jacob Grigorievich Kreizer, commander of the Soviet Far East Military Area, is a good example of a Jew placed in his present position by a chauvinistic and anti-Semitic part of the Soviet establishment. Mr. Chakovsky is one of the leading members of the anti-liberal wing of the Writers' Union in Moscow which counts many anti-Semites among its members. This can be taken as evidence that even Soviet anti-Semites are sensitive to the charge of being anti-Semitic, and put up a Jew of their own ilk to 'prove' otherwise."[23]

A Teacher's Story

One of the most dramatic stories concerning education that we heard came from a teacher who, as a girl, escaped death at the hands of the Nazis by hiding in a hayloft until her native land in Eastern Europe was liberated by the Red Army.

She was sent to the Soviet Union, where a Jewish family adopted her. At the appropriate time, she was registered with a passport stamped "Yevrei," since both parents were Jews. She became a language specialist and married a Jewish architect. Both were gifted in their fields, but found ceilings placed on their advancement. The wife was permitted to teach only in a high school despite credentials that qualified her for university status. Similar restrictions faced her husband, who, in addition, and unlike his colleagues, could not attend international conferences outside the Soviet Union.

Their applications for an apartment larger than the 66×56 feet they shared with two other couples were constantly refused.

One day she learned that her nationality card could be changed by listing a Soviet satellite country as her place of birth, and officially rejecting her adopted parents. A year after she made the change, a university post came her way, and the couple also obtained a new and larger apartment. Since then, the husband also received a better position. The woman said this was the only course open to her, but that she remembered the Jewish teachings of her adopted parents and longed to learn more about Jewish literature, history and Israel.

VI

The Economic Trials

One of the most serious Soviet attacks against Jews occurred in 1961 when the party found it convenient to cast Russian Jews in the role of principal offenders in a series of economic trials. At a time when Khrushchev's agricultural experiments were faltering and the value of the ruble was declining, delinquencies were discovered among local and state officials who allegedly were trying to enrich themselves illegally. To stem the tide of embezzlement, the death penalty was reactivated for economic offenses. The party mobilized local and national machinery, including the KGB; wholesale investigations were followed by widespread arrests, and, once again, the Jew found himself the scapegoat.

Terror stricken, the community cowered as Jews were taken before officials for inquisitory interrogation about their incomes, and some were detained overnight as questioning continued. Informers had a field day, and even schoolchildren were encouraged to report any expensive purchases made by their parents.[1] The trials represented "Soviet justice" at its worst. Frequently, the accused stood "convicted" in the newspapers alone. Even Alexander Fyodorovich Gorkin, Chairman of the U.S.S.R. Supreme Court, was moved to state that "the press sometimes publishes articles that, before hearing of a case in court, pronounce various persons guilty and prejudice the question of punishment, mostly in favor of the maximum punishment."[2]

From 1961 to 1964 more than two hundred convictions carrying the death penalty were reported. Fifty-five per cent of these were Jews; in the Ukraine the figure was 80 per cent. Whenever a Jewish identity was in doubt, the press would resort to describing the accused as the father of Lieb, or the son of Jacob or Eve, or the daughter of Aaron.

Despite international alarm and outrage, Harold J. Berman, professor of law at Harvard College, interviewed during his fifth Russian trip, told Novosti in Moscow that Soviet law still seemed to him to have been liberalized. Furthermore, he rejected any anti-Semitic implications in the large number of Jewish victims.

In sharp difference were the conclusions of the International Commission of Jurists after a comprehensive staff analysis of the trials. A report in their summer 1964 quarterly found:

It is clear that there has been an insidious and sometimes subtle propaganda campaign directed against the Jewish people of the Soviet Union, specifically against those charged with economic crimes and also against the supposed general characteristic of the Jews. If reports of trials for economic crimes are even reasonably complete, the number of Jews receiving death sentences and severe terms of imprisonment is greatly disproportionate to their number as a minority group.

They have been made the target of a dangerous propaganda campaign, and Jewish participation in economic crimes has been highlighted if not actually magnified . . . The traditional activities of Jews in history—finance and commerce are not warmly welcomed in a Communist society. It is a simple matter to link the picture of the money-grubbing Jew of anti-Semitic fancy with the picture of the archvillains of capitalist cupidity.

. . . the picture painted of the moral malaise in the Soviet Union diverts attention toward Jews because the primary object of the Soviet policy is to divert attention. . . . The real truth is a veritable cancer in the vitals of ideology—capitalist corruption even within the party and local economic administration and a spectacle of amazing fortunes made quickly.[3]

The Thirty-million Ruble Robbery

Let us study a few case histories. On November 11, 1961, *Izvestia* carried a brief story of a thirty-million-ruble robbery involving a ring of embezzlers, including fifty-four government officials in Frunze, Kirghizia. The accused were charged with operating a number of knitwear and weaving factories and absconding with huge quantities of the state's goods and public properties. The indictment charged twenty-one high-ranking directors and ministers in government offices of stealing sums ranging from 34,000 to 150,000 rubles. Despite the obvious involvement of these men, newspaper accounts made only a limited mention of their criminal acts and, instead, provided lurid details of the participation of the twenty-six Jewish defendants.

Sevetskaya Kirghizia of January 9, 1962 stated:

The whole thing started when M. Goldman, Natanson, Singer and others established a ring of embezzlers of state and public property, first at the former Frunze City Manufactured Goods Combine, which was later reorganized as the Alamedinsk Knitwear and Weaving Factory. At the end of 1955, upon the initiative of Feldscher, Stramwasser, Katz and others, a similar ring of embezzlers appeared at the Miscellaneous Manufactured Goods Co-operative, which was later reorganized as the 42nd Anniversary of October Factory: subsequently M. Goldman, Singer, Feldscher, Stramwasser, Katz and others entered into a compact, and this is how large gangs of embezzlers sprouted at these factories and operated for a number of years.

The materials of the investigation show that this was embezzling organized to the ultimate degree. The embezzlers' gang was composed of several groups. Their duties included obtaining and buying equipment and raw and other materials, marketing finished goods, bribing officials to obtain their help in securing scarce raw materials and equipment and marketing finished goods, etc. Feldscher headed one of these groups at the 42nd Anniversary of October Plant and Talasbayev headed one at the Alamedinsk Factory. For example, Feldscher, Talasbayev, Goldman and Gerber established contacts with officials through whom raw materials and equipment could be obtained. Katz, Singer, Stramwasser and others recruited for the shops reliable persons to produce "unreported" goods. Gasenfrants, Gerber, Stramwasser and others traveled from city to city and gave bribes to their spiritual brethren, who in return shipped raw materials and machine tools to Frunze.[4]

Another article in the same paper a few weeks later dramatized the "ruthlessness" of the criminals who allegedly sought to bribe state officials to join in their criminal acts:

As the judicial process determined, one of the leaders of the plundering band, M. Goldman, who was chief of the knitted-goods shop, had been stealing state property with his brother U. Goldman for a number of years. Goldman acquired low-quality raw materials by illegal means and sent them on to be manufactured as finished goods. High-quality raw materials were used in the manufacture of goods of the so-called "unaccounted" variety, which were sold with the aid of commercial workers Natanson, Taubas, Zelenaza, Alterman and Aspis. The proceeds from these sales were appropriated by Goldman and his accomplices. In the Rayon Commercial Combine . . . bookkeeping and security were paralyzed because of the fraud and misappropriation . . . So, step by step, the mass of monstrous crimes is being investigated. Goldman, Gasenfrants, Talasbayev, Gerber, Natanson, Dyushaliev, Aspis, Farlandskii and others have stolen more than thirty million rubles in government funds. . . .[5]

The Frunze affair raised a question. Why were there so many Jewish defendants? The 1959 census found so few Jews in the Kirghiz Republic that they were not even listed among national minorities residing in the republic. Although stressing the lurid details of criminal activities, the newspaper accounts failed to enumerate a number of facts. The initial story named fifty-four defendants, while another article listed forty-six individuals, mentioning that other unnamed persons were charged. Another article, two months later, listed only forty-four persons, reporting that others had been prosecuted, but failing to explain the discrepancy in numbers.

One individual, A. Greenberg (alias Pramberg), appears in the first newspaper account, disappears in subsequent accounts, and in the final story announcing the sentences, he is listed as receiving a fifteen-year prison term in addition to having his property confiscated. The final article listed by name nine defendants receiving death sentences and added that unnamed others received the same sentence. The same pattern was applied to those receiving prison terms.

The discrepancies in the court records and newspaper accounts had the staff of the International Commission of Jurists wondering how in such a tightly controlled totalitarian system could an operation of the magnitude of the Frunze affair have ever been established without the full co-operation of government officials. Furthermore they said, "the prominence given to the Jewish defendants clearly indicates an attempt to lay the main guilt at their door."[6]

Basia Reznicky, a Jew from Vilna, became the first woman since Stalin's time to receive the death sentence. Her husband, Aaron, and Fedor Kaminer, Mikhail Rabinovich (all of whom received the death penalty) and four others were found guilty of currency speculation. The case received careful propaganda treatment in *Pravda, Izvestia* and *Komsomolskaya Pravda* and attracted wide public attention. The accused were reported to have carried out their illegal manipulations in the local synagogue and trafficked with Jewish speculators in many other cities. The *Pravda* report characterized the defendants as "people standing apart from life and not interested in how the Soviet people lived."

Basia Reznicky's brothers living in Israel and the United States were frequently mentioned by the newspapers. The pattern of linking illicit Jewish activities to the synagogue, and of casting doubts on their loyalty by mentioning relatives abroad, became prominent in a number of cases during this period.

Other "Criminal" Cases

Jews were charged even with dealing in gold coins. Another case cited concerned three Moscow Jews sentenced for baking and selling matzos illegally, and three Jews in Piatigorsk Stavropol, including a Rabbi Gavrilov, who were sentenced to death for trading in gold and foreign currencies.

Jewish defendants in Khmelnitskyi, the Ukraine, were found guilty merely of handling the gold coins of a man named Poisner and a currency dealer, Kuris. Another story tells how a Dr. S. Grossman, in the resort of Sernovodsk-Kavkazsky, built two houses for himself on government property with state funds and labor.

A mass trial occurred in Kiev in December 1962. Six Jewish warehouse workers and commodity experts employed by the fruit and vegetable trust were listed as the principal defendants, charged with fraud and embezzlement. According to the indictment, they had adulterated the grade of goods delivered to the pickling factory and had pocketed the difference in prices obtained from the consumer. The six received harsh penalties, leaving many to wonder how these individuals, apparently lacking professional backgrounds, were able to issue false papers, invoices and documents without the help of government employees.

Alster Bronshtein, 81, the central figure in a trial in Chernovtsy involving fifteen defendants, was depicted by

Pravda Ukrainy as ". . . pretending poverty. He would go into the cafeterias, look hastily about and eat the leftovers on tables, stuffing the pockets of his threadbare coat with pieces of bread. He engaged in begging." A second speculator, Yefim Margoshes, was chastised for taking advantage of the state after receiving a free education and entering a profession. But, the paper said, "Yefim was a scoundrel. He did not have it in him to do honest work, and as a railway inspector he used every opportunity to establish connections with the criminal underworld." A third person, Moishe-Meyer Zayats, was described as "speculating in everything from women's stockings to gold."

To assure Ukrainians that Soviet justice was tempered with mercy, the writer mentioned that one of the accused, a Jewish woman, had been released. Had not the court decided to free her, the woman's young child would have been without a mother. Readers were asked to speculate on the wisdom of this action, for the woman, left without "capitalistic wealth," became so distraught that she never properly cared for her child and even attempted suicide. Six of the others, all Jews, were sentenced to death.

Repeated reports in the Western press of various show trials and stories singling out Jews as chief offenders in these economic offenses aroused Jews and the non-Jewish community throughout the world. Soviet counterpropaganda shrugged off the mounting protests and criticisms with the same excuses that Chairman Khrushchev gave to President Eisenhower and Jewish leaders during a 1959 visit to the United States—that Soviet Jews were treated as everyone else was, and that the whole business was an internal matter. But the grim and bloody fact of the executions remained.

The Concern of the late Bertrand Russell

One of the greatest champions of the Russian Jews during this period turned out to be a friend of the Soviet Union, the late Lord Bertrand Russell. The late Martin Buber had convinced the British philosopher of the plight of the Jews. Early in 1962, the two, joined by the French writer François Mauriac, sent Khrushchev a telegram questioning the reports on economic trials. Receiving no reply, Lord Russell continuously mentioned the problem in correspondence with the Soviet leader. On February 28, 1963, *Pravda, Izvestia* and Moscow radio made public an exchange of communications between Lord Russell and Khrushchev. The Russians hoped that the persuasive response by the Soviet Premier to such a prominent figure as Russell would help to silence critics. They did not anticipate the reaction of Soviet citizens who were startled to learn that such an important progressive friend in the West showed concern about developments in their homeland.

Reports of Western alarm at the economic trials had filtered through the propaganda barrier, yet this was the first official admission that such criticism existed. The prominence given the Russell-Khrushchev exchanges served to subdue the disquiet among certain Soviet intellectuals regarding the wave of trials and its Jewish victims.

Here is what Bertrand Russell first wrote:

Dear Premier Khrushchev,

I am deeply perturbed at the death sentence passed on Jews in the Soviet Union and the official encouragement of anti-Semitism which apparently takes place. I am writing about this in a private capacity. You of course know that I am a friend of your country, and that I have a friendly attitude towards your personal efforts directed to peaceful coexistence, efforts which I have publicly supported. I appeal to you for an amnesty, proceeding from humane considerations and our joint interests, which consist in peaceful relations between East and West.

> *With respect,*
> *Yours sincerely,*
> Bertrand Russell

February 2, 1963

And this was the Soviet Premier's answer:

Esteemed Bertrand Russell.

I have received your letter in which you express alarm over the fact that among those who have lately been punished under the laws of the Soviet Union for committing crimes, termed in the Western press "economic crimes," there are people of Jewish nationality. Some people in the West describe this as a manifestation of anti-Semitism. I must tell you frankly that I am surprised by such a conclusion. It derives from a profound delusion.

In the past few months the Western bourgeois press has again been clamouring about so-called anti-Semitism in the U.S.S.R. With full responsibility for my words I declare that this is a crude concoction, a vicious slander on the Soviet people, on our country. Even the bourgeois press itself admits that there have been people of most diverse nationalities among those convicted in the U.S.S.R. for so-called "economic crimes." This is really so. People who misappropriate public property, who live in idleness out of other people's work, are convicted in our country strictly according to the existing laws. The punishment for everyone committing a crime is determined by the nature of that particular crime and, of course, has nothing to do with his nationality. . . .

. . . It is well known that bourgeois propaganda often resorts to slander and falsification in order to vilify our socialist system and our morals, in an effort to vilify our system and its laws. They resort to the method of attributing to it, with ill intent, features allegedly directed against a particular nationality—the Jewish nationality—but this is easily refuted by facts. It is not difficult to find proof, even in the records of trials published in newspapers, that among those punished by our courts for what is called "economic crimes," including those sentenced to capital punishment, there are Russians and Jews, Georgians and Ukrainians, Byelorussians and people of other nationalities. . . .

We appreciate, Mr. Russell, your friendly sentiments for our country. We understand that your letter has been prompted by humanitarian considerations. But humanity is inconceivable without justice, and it is precisely in the interests of justice that our people must punish those who want to live at the expense of others and to pillage our society.

The attempts by reactionary propaganda to impute a policy of anti-Semitism, or encouragement of it, to our state is not a new feature. The class enemies in the past, too, more than once resorted to such slander against our reality, against our order. There never has been and there is not any policy of anti-Semitism in the Soviet Union, since the very nature of our multinational socialist state precludes the possibility of such a policy. Our constitution proclaims the equality of the citizens of the U.S.S.R., irrespective of their nationality and race, and declares that "any advocacy of racial or national exclusiveness or hatred or contempt is punishable by law."

The motto of our society proclaims: man is to man a friend, comrade and brother. We have always educated and continue to educate the Soviet people in a spirit of friendship and brotherhood of all peoples, in a spirit of intolerance for national and racial enmity. You may rest assured that we shall continue to do this with utmost persistence and consistence.

Respectfully yours,
Nikita Khrushchev

21st February, 1963.
(reprinted from *Jews in Eastern Europe,* May 1963)

Lord Russell was not satisfied. On March 5, another two-page letter was sent to the Russian leader. The British philosopher had divided the half-truths and gratuitous explanations in the Premier's answer. Statistical charts showed the disproportionate number of Jewish victims compared with other nationalities. Furthermore, Khrushchev's remark, "There never has been and there is not any policy of anti-Semitism in the Soviet Union, since the very nature of our multinational socialist state precludes the possibility of such a policy," had all the earmarks of Stalin terrorism and were glaringly false.

The correspondence from a renowned world intellectual and champion of socialist causes produced a wave of discussions inside the Soviet Union. Obviously anxious about the rumblings aroused by the Khrushchev-Russell letters, *Izvestia* printed four reactions extracted from an alleged two hundred letters from readers. A Jew from Lvov, one L. Rozman, asked how he could be named chairman of his trade union under anti-Semitism. He favored punishment handed down to criminals against the state saying, "People were shot not because they were

Jews, but because they committed against the people severe criminal acts." A driver from Sverdlovsk named Berukhovitch reminded Russell of the suffering of the Jews under Tsarist regimes: "Why raise the issue now and ascribe it to the new Soviet Russia? How could my children be an English teacher, a medical student and a student military specialist if this was so?"

Finally a Leningrad lathe operator, S. Krestin, wrote:

Dear philosopher, how deeply in error you are concerning our reality, and then what would one of your common citizens think about it? For you have better opportunities to establish the truth: you, certainly, follow our press, meet our prominent people, and, finally, can come and look with your own eyes at Soviet life. Try asking Soviet Jews if they would like another regime. Such a question could insult anybody.[7]

On April 6, 1963, Lord Russell sent *Izvestia* his reaction to the letters-to-the-editor. After nearly three months of unsuccessful attempts to have the letter published, Russell released the letter in London.

From The Earl Russell, O.M., F.R.S.,
6 April 1963

To The Editor of *Izvestia:*
Dear Sir,

I am pleased to see that the letter written by Premier Khrushchev to me concerning the condition of Soviet Jews was published in *Izvestia* along with one of the letters I have written on this subject to Mr. Khrushchev. I have also read with genuine interest the readers' letters which comment on our correspondence. I am sympathetic to what they say of the achievements of the Soviet Union with regard to the abolition of legal disabilities imposed on Jews during the Czarist days. This is a matter of special interest to me because my grandfather was responsible for the elimination of legal discrimination against Jews in Great Britain.

I am a friend of the Soviet Union, of her people and of her desire to improve and advance the conditions under which her citizens live. I am an ardent campaigner for close and genuinely co-operative relations between the people and governments of Western countries and the Soviet Union. I am a passionate opponent of the cold war and of all attempts to increase hostility, exploit differences and add to the terrible dangers facing mankind today. I know that no Soviet citizen will misunderstand me or think that when I speak frankly I wish to harm the Soviet Union or co-operate with those who promote the cold war.

One of the tests of true friendship is the ability to speak frankly without fear of being taken for an enemy or of being misunderstood. I hope, therefore, that you will appreciate the spirit in which I am now writing—one of concern for the Soviet people and not a spirit of condemnation.

The Jews have been subjected to a long and continuous persecution in the history of Europe. The culmination of this cruelty was the wholesale extermination of millions of Jews during our lifetimes, one of the most barbaric crimes in all human history. If ever a people were deserving of understanding and sympathetic treatment after harsh suffering, it is the Jews of Europe.

I should hope, therefore, that the Jews would be permitted full cultural lives, religious freedom and the rights of a national group, in practice as well as in law.

During the last years of Stalin's life, Soviet Jews were totally deprived of their national culture and the means of expressing it. Leading intellectuals were imprisoned or executed by extralegal practices which have since been condemned.

I am a lifelong non-believer in any religion. I have written and campaigned against superstition. Nonetheless, I believe that the freedom to practise religious views should be allowed

Jews of the Soviet Union in the same manner that such freedom is granted people of other religious persuasion. I am concerned that the process of restitution of much smaller groups are more plentiful and the closure of synagogues and shortage of religious facilities have impaired Jews in the pursuit of their beliefs. I am troubled that there should be articles in Soviet journals of many Republics expressing hostility of Jewish people as such.

I understand the objections to economic offenses such as were expressed in the letter to me by Premier Khrushchev. I feel, however, that the death penalty upon citizens accused of these crimes harms the Soviet Union and allows those hostile to her to unjustly malign her. I consider the fact that 60 per cent of those executed are Jews to be gravely disturbing. I fervently hope that nothing will take place which obliges us to believe that Jews are receiving unjust treatment in contradiction to the law, and that those who break Soviet laws concerning economic offences will be rehabilitated instead of being put to death. I cannot too strongly appeal for understanding of the difficulty experienced by those in the West who are working dedicatedly to ease tension, promote peaceful co-existence, and to end the cold war. These objects are harmed by events which those who desire the cold war can exploit and which trouble us who wish peace and good relations. I write as a friend, but one whose friendship requires honesty.

Yours sincerely,
Bertrand Russell

(*Jews in Eastern Europe,* September 1963)

"No Mercy for Thieves"

Determined to prove to the world the fairness of Soviet justice, *Izvestia* heralded the coming of a special "show trial to demonstrate that economic sabotage is a form of

ideological subversion of Soviet society." Two Jews,
Shakerman and Roifman, were said to be the ringleaders
of a gang stealing more than thirty million rubles over a
period of years, until their activities were unearthed by
the KGB. If this case seems like the one just preceding,
it is not a repetition but a resemblance in the traditional
Soviet manner of reiterating stock charges and even du-
plicating a *modus operandi*. Close Russian-watchers say
that identical charges in nearly identical language are
used periodically when thought necessary, as if the pros-
ecuting individuals had the benefit of a standing library
of condemnation to resort to. It is not unusual for the
U.S.S.R. to produce the same smash hit with different
casts of characters year in and year out in the hinterlands,
on their off-Broadway and on their Great White Way
itself. In an article, "There Will Be No Mercy for
Thieves," Yu. Feofanov, an editor of *Izvestia*, departed
from the usual procedure of identifying Jews only by
forenames or patronymics, and by mentioning one's religious practices or by subtly stressing Jewish characteristics of the accused. "These acts are a dreadful, heinous
crime against the Soviet state, against every Soviet citizen," the writer said, demanding a widely publicized
trial to be prosecuted by the U.S.S.R.'s Procurator-
General. "We mention the Jewish surnames because we
pay no heed to the malicious slander that is stirred up
from time to time in the Western press. It is not Jews,
Russians, Tartars or Ukrainians who will stand trial:
Criminals will stand trial."

According to *Izvestia*, Shakerman had had his eye on
the wife of a distant relative. He offered the relative a

huge sum of money to get out of the way and leave him free to marry the lady. At first, the relative agreed. After thinking the matter over, he changed his mind and called in the local KGB man who went to the culprit's apartment and discovered 316,000 rubles, several pounds of gold and other valuables. A visit to Roifman's quarters unearthed another fortune. How did they do it? The inventive Roifman had bribed his way to the position of manager of an occupational-therapy workshop attached to a psychoneurological center in Moscow. There, he and accomplices on the staff bribed members of the Soviet economic police and supervisory trade organizations to set up a knitwear factory at the cost of 178,000 rubles. They established trade relations with fifty-two factories, artisan co-operatives and shops. Then, using fifty-eight machines and four hundred and sixty tons of wool, they manufactured fashionable knitwear. They sold them at Moscow's railway station, under the eyes of the state officials. "Hoorah," *Izvestia* cried out, "to our Chekists of KGB for exposing this ideological subversion directed against our society. Imagine how many kindergartens, clinics and cafeterias could have been built with the stolen thirty millions of currency, gold, diamonds and platinum. WE DEMAND PUNISHMENT FOR THE ROBBERS . . . COMPLETE WITH SUPREME PENALTY FOR THE RINGLEADERS."[8] If Soviet citizens were waiting for further news about the public trial, they had to be content with a brief report in January that the trial was in progress and with a final announcement a month later that nine persons, six of them Jews, had been sentenced to death, while fourteen received prison terms ranging up to fifteen years each.

The New York *Times* reported that "plans for the show trial were shelved, presumably because of the involvement of bribetaking Soviet officials." Furthermore, the newspaper said, Western newsmen, outsiders and visitors were barred from the courtroom "because the bribetakers were to be identified during testimony."[9]

If the Stalin purges failed to arouse world opinion to the plight of the three million, the economic trials accomplished the feat. No doubt exists that world protests prevented a continuation of such trials.

Recently, world Jewry became alarmed, as an economic-crime trial, held in 1968, sentenced some fourteen defendants to death. Most of the accused were Jewish. The Soviet Law Journal indicated that more trials lay ahead, with about eighty people suspected of similar large-scale speculations and embezzlements. The March 13, 1969 issue of *Sovietskaya Rossiya* cited four Leningrad Jews among many defendants charged with embezzling government goods in a textile plant. The journal's report named four Jewish individuals as having received sentences from six to fourteen years and added, "others were sentenced to various terms."

One cannot say whether this type of Soviet justice will repeat itself but as *Time* magazine stated in its November 10, 1967 issue, "In the courts, the regime lately takes more care to keep an outward show of legality, but it easily ignores the law when convenient; the party, after all, is above the law."

Figure 5. Digging in.

Figure 6.

В РОКИ ГІТЛЕРІВСЬКОЇ ОКУПАЦІЇ ВЕРХОВОДИ-СІО-
НІСТИ ПРИСЛУЖУВАЛИ ФАШИСТАМ

Figure 7. During the years of the Hitlerite occupation, the
Zionist leaders served the Fascists.

VII
Israel and the U.S.S.R.

Almost within hours after the defeat in 1967 of the Russian-supported Arab armies by Israel, the U.S.S.R.'s anti-Israel, anti-Jewish propaganda campaign took a new turn as Kremlin leaders sought to turn military defeat into propaganda victory.

Intensification of Anti-Semitism

In a frontal attack that blanketed the world through the press, radio and television, international broadcasts, and forums like the United Nations, the Soviet Union's official statements suddenly became violently anti-Semitic. Western observers of all stripe were shocked by articles using slanderous and vitriolic language such as this statement that appeared in *Sovietskaya Latvia* on August 5, 1967:

A wide network of Zionist organizations with a common center, a common program and funds exceeding by far the funds of the Mafia "Cosa Nostra" is active behind the scenes of international theater. Zionism is not an obsolete term by any means. Zionism was and is to this day a dangerous weapon of the imperialistic West, an enemy of all workers of all nationalities.

In the same way that synagogue Jews were depicted as criminals and currency speculators, this latest comparison of Zionism and Israel with the most notorious international crime syndicate automatically condemned world Jewry, not just the Russian Jew. As one diplomat noted in August 1967: "It's going to be hard to convince some latent anti-Semite in the Ukraine or Byelorussia that this isn't the signal to let himself go."[1]

Russian Jews, still remembering the terror of Stalin and the economic trials, were horrified that the word Zionism suddenly became freely associated with anti-Semitism. The average Christian has difficulty in understanding the Jewish organizational structure, its religious branches and its people as an ethnic group. The sharp delineation between Israelis and Jews has been made primarily by Jews of the Diaspora who identify with the country of their residence. Therefore, for the Russian peasants, unexposed to the intellectual forums of the West, this type of distinction is practically impossible. Having lived all their lives with the tradition of anti-Semitism, they cannot comprehend the difference between the Jewish people, Zionism and Judaism.

Abraham Brumberg, the editor of the bimonthly journal, *Problems of Communism,* told a plenary session of the National Community Relations Advisory Council in Atlantic City in July 1967, the "phantasmagoric nature of this most recent campaign is evident in the two constantly recurring themes found in many Soviet articles and broadcasts. The first of these is the allegation that Israel and Zionism are the tools for United States imperialism. The second, and more important, is their blatant comparison of Israeli military tactics with those used by the Nazis in World War II." He told the Jewish leaders that this is especially typified "in the rash of cartoons that have appeared in the Soviet press, portraying hook-nosed Israeli soldiers with blood dripping from their hands, committing unspeakable crimes . . ."[2] (Fig. 2) The Soviet press accused the Israelis of atrocities against women, children and prisoners. Just how vicious this campaign was, can be seen in these samples taken from Soviet press and radio broadcasts:

In the Sinai Peninsula, unarmed Egyptian soldiers were driven to the West by Israeli tanks. Those who were not fast enough or were exhausted, perished under the tank tracks . . . Refugees said that all who refused to leave the villages were shot by the occupiers. Many inhabitants of Hashaya were killed in a mosque.

Israeli aircraft bombed hospitals and motor ambulances carrying wounded from the battlefields. The invaders fired in cold blood against soldiers with their hands up . . . The inhabitants of the Syrian village of Mansourah were put in a house and after having soaked it with gasoline the Israelis set fire to it . . . The militarist elite in Tel Aviv . . . gave orders to its troops not to take prisoners. And obeying this cannibalistic order, the Israeli tanks ran over disarmed men, while aircraft machine-gunned them in low-level flight.[3]

And on June 16, an *Izvestia* correspondent filed the following story from Rome based on an interview with an unnamed Italian reporter just returned from covering the war:

Israeli troops poured gasoline over the live bodies of Arab prisoners of war and set them on fire . . . I cannot help comparing the Jewish girl Anne Frank, who was tortured to death by the Hitlerites and whose dramatic diary shook the whole world, with General Dayan, whose actions have surpassed those of the inhuman Nazis!

In little more than two decades, the U.S.S.R.'s policy toward Israel has made a complete turnabout, Brumberg told the Jewish leaders of the NCRAC. Furthermore, he said, "The attacks on American behavior in Vietnam have seldom reached such heights of vituperation. This propaganda reminds one uncomfortably more of the indecent absurdities of the Protocols of the Elders of Zion than of even the most obnoxious political polemics."

Indeed, the authorities could not have chosen a more hurtful, more slanderous theme for attacking a people who lost six million compatriots to Nazi bestiality. (Fig. 3) Poland and other Red-block nations echoed the party line. Ida Kaminska, Academy Award nominee for her role in *The Shop on Main Street*, and members of her National Yiddish Theatre Company became victims of the Polish drive. After returning from a triumphant visit to New York, Mrs. Kaminska quickly sensed the changing climate in Poland. Her daughter, Ruth, recalled how conditions appeared similar to those in the Soviet Union. She said Polish authorities forbade Mrs. Kaminska from representing her country at the Czechoslovakia film festival in Carlsbad. They prevented her husband, Marion Melman, from going to East Germany to dub a film he had completed. The Polish authorities charged the actress and her company with having conducted a pro-Zionist propaganda campaign during their United States tour and denied the theatrical company further rights for overseas performances. This action prompted Mrs. Kaminska and her family to join the thousands of departing Polish Jews. It is interesting to note that Poland places no restrictions on Jewish emigration.

The postwar propaganda attack served as both a catalyst and shock treatment for spurring Western Jewish action. Those still stressing differences between the U.S.S.R.'s anti-Jewish statements and political attacks against Israel quickly dropped their objections. Many suddenly came to the realization that not only had the Soviet-backed Arabs threatened the possible extinction of two million Israelis but that their three million brethren in the U.S.S.R. faced grave dangers.

The Ancient "Enemy"—Zionism

The Soviet struggle against Zionism, and its distrust of Jews did not begin, of course, with the Six Day war. Zionism perturbed the Communists at its very outset, since its creed of nationalism and call for a Jewish homeland sharply differed from the Marx-Engels doctrine of socialist universalism. Lenin offered different solutions for settling the Jewish question, but still called the Zionist philosophy counterrevolutionary and in conflict with the interests of the Jewish proletariat.

At the turn of the century, Russian Zionism, even though outlawed and forced underground by the Tsar, proved itself one of the most vital forces on the international scene and produced some of the future architects of the state of Israel. By the time the Bolsheviks seized power, there were 1200 Zionist organizations in Russia with a total membership of 300,000. Zionist cultural and educational activities served as an important community organ, exemplified by thirty-nine Yiddish, ten Hebrew and three Russian periodicals. Commissar Semen M. Dimanshtain tried to woo Russian Zionists with slogans of "a Palestine in Moscow"[4] based on new labor communes which he said would be far more suitable under Bolshevik socialism than under British imperialism. One of the objectives for the Jewish settlement in Birobizhan was to further the regime's desire to win over Jewish masses while dealing a deadly blow to Zionism.

gandists. On September 1, 1919, the Cheka, the secret police (later called the KGB) raided Zionist offices in Leningrad, Moscow and other centers, confiscating documents and money, arresting leaders and achieving their prime objective of stilling the voice of Zionist periodicals. In the latter part of 1922, thousands of Zionist leaders were imprisoned in a series of wholesale arrests. A handful succumbed to pressure, and in exchange for exit permits to Palestine, signed confessions stating that Zionist goals were anti-Soviet and contrary to revolutionary objectives.

Despite these acts of suppression, the movement remained 30,000 strong.

The UN and the Creation of Israel

When the United Nations passed the Palestine partition resolution, Moscow radio blared that "The Soviet Union is the only true friend of Jewish national independence. The United States merely pretended friendship with Israel. The act of aggression was being waged by the Arab legions (against Israel) with the aid of America and Great Britain." (Fig. 4) So convinced were the Arab leaders of Kremlin assistance to Israel that Dr. Ibrahim Al-Shuraiky wrote in *Al Hayat:* "The creation of the new nation was a Soviet plot conceived by Lenin and carried out by Stalin."

At the United Nations on May 14, 1947, the U.S.S.R.'s chief United Nations delegate fought off British and American objections in pleading for the creation of a Jewish homeland:

During the last war (in Europe), the Jewish people underwent exceptional sorrow and suffering. Without any exaggeration, this sorrow and suffering is indescribable. It is difficult to express it in dry statistics of the Jewish victims of the Fascist aggressors. The Jews in territories where the Hitlerites held sway were subjected to almost complete annihilation. The total number of members of the Jewish population who perished at the hands of Nazi executioners is estimated at approximately six million. Only about a million and a half Jews in Western Europe survived the war . . .

The fact that no Western European state has been able to ensure the defense of the elementary rights of the Jewish people, and to safeguard it against the violence of the Fascist executioners, explains the aspirations of the Jews to establish their own state. It would be unjust not to take this into consideration and to deny the right of the Jewish people to realize this aspiration. . . .[5]

Soviet leaders find nothing irrational by one day at home combating Zionism and the next day pleading for the Herzl dream. "As far as the Soviet Union is concerned, there is only one kind of logic in foreign affairs: The

logic of what is best for the Soviet Union,"[6] Gromyko
once asserted. After the historic UN vote creating Israel,
the Soviet Union became the first government granting
official recognition to the new state. In 1948 as Jews
staved off Arab legions, Gromyko led the fight for a series
of UN cease-fires at the United Nations. During this
time the Soviet Union defied the arms-embargo agree-
ment to send munition supplies to the Israeli fighters.
Armed with new Czech machine guns and rifles, Mes-
serschmidts and Spitfires, the Israelis held firm in their
battle for their part of Jerusalem as the tide turned in
their favor. The Russians even helped the Israelis train
to use the new Czech planes. One such recruit was
Mordecai Hod who, nineteen years later as the commander of Israel's air force, commanded the destruction
of the Russian-equipped Egyptian air force.[7]

Turn-About-Face

It didn't take long for traditional fears of Zionism and
dual Jewish loyalty to change the Kremlin's tune, for
when Mrs. Golda Meir arrived in Moscow in July 1948,
as the first Israeli envoy, she was greeted by hundreds
of emigration applications from Russian Jews. On October 16, Mrs. Meir and her staff observed Rosh Hashanah
at Moscow's Central Synagogue. She was greeted by an
overflow of more than 10,000 people. Large banners with
"Israel Is Born," inscribed in Hebrew, draped the con-
gregational walls. As Mrs. Meir made her way into the
sanctuary, hands reached out to touch her sleeve or
dress. Those who got close enough kissed her shawl as
if they were embracing the Torah.

A New York *Herald Tribune* reporter described the event as unprecedented in more than thirty years of Communist rule. "Men and women cried," he wrote, "and, as Mrs. Meir and the Israeli party walked back to the hotel, the crowd followed for one more glimpse, shouting '*Am Yisroel Hai*' (the people of Israel lives). The Israeli official was deeply touched and said 'I choked with emotion and could hardly contain the tears from flowing . . .'"

Ten days later, on Yom Kippur, the same enthusiasm was displayed. The government could not permit such a show of nationalistic fervor. It might arouse others. The fire had to be put out. The late Illya Ehrenburg wrote an article for *Pravda* condemning Zionists as mystics. Avowing Russia's sympathy with the new state, he told Jews that their solution, nevertheless, lay in the development of socialism in their countries of residence, rather than in the creation of a new nation. A hard line toward Zionism was resumed. Young men expressing interest in Israel were interrogated and frequently arrested.

The Split

When 1949 arrived, the honeymoon between Israel and the U.S.S.R. was over. By 1952 the Soviet line was that Israel had been created by the "imperialists and colonialists," leaving the majority of Arabs to believe that the formation of Israel was wholly engineered by the West. The Soviet army paper, *Red Star*, attacked a United States loan of 100 million dollars to Israel as anti-Russian, "aimed at converting the Middle East into a military base for Anglo-American imperialism and a springboard to attack the U.S.S.R."[8] (Fig. 5) Realizing the new nation would now never become a "cold-war" partner, Stalin utilized the bombing of the Soviet delegation in Tel Aviv (said by some to have been engineered by the Russians) to sever diplomatic relations on February 12, 1953.

Diplomatic relations between the two countries were resumed on July 20, 1953, under the regime of Georgi Malenkov, but his successor, Nikita S. Khrushchev, drastically altered the Kremlin's Middle East policy in favor of the Arabs.

The Kremlin propagandists seized upon this new posture to paint a bleak portrait of life in Israel, a ploy to discourage any Soviet Jew from even visiting his relatives or holding thoughts of emigration. Israeli diplomats were carefully watched and anyone contacting a member of their diplomatic staff could expect a thorough going-over by police officials. (When I met with the Israeli ambassador at our Moscow hotel, he suggested we talk in the garden to prevent unfriendly ears from eavesdropping in the lobby.) Scores of articles appeared, like the alleged confessions of seventy-five-year-old Zelman Greenberg, who had left for Israel to join his daughter in Haifa after a separation of twenty years.

It was the darkest and worst day of my life . . . something was not as it should be in this "earthly paradise for Jews." . . . I have looked more closely and have understood. You cannot hope for more than bread and water. I say this not to make it sound better—it really is so. In the morning before work begins they have for breakfast radish and tea, something cheaper cannot be found. They take with them a piece of bread—and what bread: the cheapest bread for eighteen agarot, which is mixed with all you want. Good bread in this house, if you can find it, is only for Saturdays and holidays. At times my daughter and son-in-law buy a bit of sour milk for the bread and this is all they eat. In the evening when they come home, their dinner consists of fried carrots, with a little cheap flour and oil.

And so it is every day. Meat is seldom on their menu. Once every week, or once in two weeks, Beila will buy two hundred grams of frozen black meat that in our house in Russia a wife would not dare serve, and for them this is a luxury. They live in a peasant hut, made from cardboard and plywood and all they possess are a folding bed, a settee, a small table, chairs and only the clothes they stood up in.[9]

On July 17, 1960, the Soviet paper *Trud* accused Israeli tourists and diplomats with "infiltrating anti-Soviet and pro-Zionist propaganda into the Soviet Union aimed at encouraging emigration to Israel." Another accusation against Israeli diplomats appeared in a Kharkov article describing the activities of the "rude, arrogant, unclean idler," Arnold Solomonovich Bogdanovsky, whose actions are pictured as "the lowest point of human degradation— the betrayer of the fatherland." The Ukrainian language article, "The Degenerate," by V. Danilov (February 9, 1966) explains how Bogdanovsky rejects the educational and employment opportunities offered by the Communist system, because "for him there exists no rules of communal living. He is very unclean in his living habits. One day in Moscow he shamed his fatherland when he rushed to the Central Synagogue to meet Aryeh Ard of the Israeli embassy to establish contact and receive favors in exchange for information. Then, the Ukrainian Jew meets his Israeli friend at the Black Sea resort of Yalta, where he is introduced to Moshe and Ora Zimrat of the Israeli embassy. Their only interest was to impose reactionary Zionist ideas on some of our people."

As mentioned in previous chapters, tourists visiting synagogues do leave religious articles for worshipers, and although official greeters deny the need for such items, the people eagerly accept such gifts. We met several tourists who asked us for extra articles of clothing for relatives. Actually, souvenir hunting has become a favorite sport in many Russian cities. Few visitors return without tales of the many ball-point pens, lipsticks or soft-cover English-language books they have given away. I remember the excitement as I passed out shiny new John F. Kennedy fifty-cent pieces to my Intourist guide, a hat-check man, a maid and a waitress. I particularly remember the face of a telephone operator in the hotel where I had spent the afternoon placing calls to Moscow. After three hours and a great deal of mutual patience, my calls were completed. In appreciation, I handed her the new coin. She grasped it and glowed as she said, *"Kyenedy, he vuz vunderful man."* In a responsive gesture she handed me a Lenin memorial ruble as a token of friendship.

The Hope That Is Israel

Israel represents a part of positive Jewishness that the Russian Jew can cling to with pride and admiration.

He manifests this in strange ways. When Israel still carried on trade relations with the U.S.S.R., Jews would
grab up Jaffa oranges sold at local fruit stands not for
the fruit, but for the tissue wrapper inscribed with Hebrew lettering which many flattened out and preserved
hidden in books. However, any Jew expressing kinship
with Israel in the Soviet Union today must do so with
utmost caution. During our visit to one community, a
younger man pressed a piece of paper into my hand
saying, "It's a poem I wrote about Israel. Please take
it back, show it to your friends." Apparently this poet
has at best had six or seven years of school. The poor
construction of his phrases and the grammatical errors
attest to this. Yet the verse bursts with personal pride
and emotion, attesting to his love for the state of Israel. Our nameless poet addresses himself to the future,
expressing the prayer of Russian Jews that the coming
generation can experience better conditions, perhaps in
Israel:

> We have erected an eternal monument
> This monument is a basis of many faiths
> Believe in this;
> O future generations, believe in this all
>   nations of earth.
> My land and my people are indivisible
> They strive to victories confidently.
> Those victories are equality and work.
> The whole planet has heard about my land.
> The smallest nation on earth knows my land.
> While at the beginning we were looked down
>   upon by the world
> But afterwards we achieved glory.
> O miracle of miracles, long wished for freedom

your brightness is an eternal
flame.
You came to shine for my people who seem to be
in an eternal sleep.
Do not forget to lay a wreath of laurels on the
tombstone of one who is clean
in soul.
Who was like a beacon for many
Who was the first of the first of Zionists.
And if in battle I have to die for my country's
ideal;
Without hesitation I would die:
So that the eternal star would shine (for
future generations).

VIII
The Work of Trofim Kitchko

Even after the Stalin purges and the infamy of the Doctors' Plot, many American Jews remained unconvinced that Russian Jews were in danger of spiritual or religious annihilation. Their energies were directed toward the succor of Israel, and matters dealing with Russian Jews were relegated primarily to three agencies: the American Jewish Committee, the American Jewish Congress, and B'nai B'rith.

The spirit of appeasement was abroad in the land. According to Philip Baum, international affairs director of the American Jewish Congress, "In the early days of the protest action, American Jews were overcautious and careful in their use of terms attacking the Russians. The fear still existed that Russian Jews would face serious reprisals if the attacks were too strong. For this reason, terms like 'anti-Jewish,' rather than 'anti-Semitic,' were preferred by many Jewish leaders in drafting speeches and statements."

Six weeks before a climactic organizational conference in Washington (see Chapter X), Jewish timidity evaporated. At a press conference, Morris B. Abram, then president of the American Jewish Committee, exhibited *Judaism Without Embellishment*, a coarse and brutal book larded with cartoons by Trofim Korneyevich Kitchko, a Ukrainian professor.

Abram held up the almost unbelievable work with its three-color cover showing a rabbinical figure covered by the traditional prayer shawl, leaning down from the pulpit, the stereotyped smile upon thick lips below the hooked nose; in its clawlike hands, the figure held a pile of gold coins. (Fig. 6)

The book, published in 1963 by the Ukrainian Academy of Sciences in an edition of 12,000 copies, claimed "to reveal to the reader the actual essence of the Jewish religion (Judaism)—one of the ancient religions of the world, which has collected within itself and condensed everything that is most reactionary and anti-humane in the writings of contemporary religions." The intention, according to the preface, was to show how "honorable Jews" were breaking away from the synagogue and the teachings of the Torah and Talmud once they understood "that they are the tools for the insidious deception of the faithful."

Kitchko, no novice to propaganda warfare, in 1957 produced for the Ukrainian Society for the Dissemination of Political and Scientific Knowledge a forty-eight-page Ukrainian language textbook called *The Jewish Religion, its Origins and Character*. This crude exercise used explanations of Jewish religious practices and Judaism as a pretext for propaganda charges against Israel, Zionism and the Jewish people:

Judaism has always served, by the nature of its creed, the plundering policy of capitalism . . . Jewish clergy have thereby actively assisted the foreign imperialists . . . Judaism has pitched the Jews against other nations . . . Zionist leaders were collaborators with Hitler in his crimes against the world.

Another Kitchko work appearing in the December 1962 issue of *Voyovnichy Ateist* in Kiev told his readers that the teachings of Judaism "are permeated by a hatred toward work and scorn of the working man, its religious teachings are filled, not with the concept of work, but with a narrow practicality . . . how to make profit, love of money and the spirit of egotism . . ."

Professor Pioter Nedbailo, Ukrainian delegate to the UN Human Rights Commission, denied that Kitchko's cartoons were anti-Semitic. Commenting on one drawing of a Jew lowering himself to lick a Nazi boot, Nedbailo said the picture merely depicted a quisling character. "We all had our quislings. There were Ukrainian quislings and Jewish quislings. This shows a Jewish quisling." (Fig. 7)

World opinion differed. "Only the Nazis were so vulgar," said the Swedish Social Democrat newspaper, *Aftonbladt.* Olof Starkenberg, foreign editor of that nation's liberal newspaper, *Expressen,* said: "Not since the time of the disgusting Jew-baiter Julius Streicher has anything comparable been published, in words or picture." Western Communists were equally critical of the work. Even U. S. Communist Party boss Gus Hall said, "There is no doubt in my mind about the anti-Semitic character of what I have seen. Such stereotyped, slanderous caricatures of the Jewish people must be unequivocally condemned."

At first, the Russians defended the Kitchko book. The Novosti Press Agency sent a reply through the French

Jewish (Yiddish) Communist organ *Naie Presse*, signed by a Soviet Jew, Schimon Katz. The article claimed the Ukrainian author merely conducted himself as a good Soviet citizen by carrying out the mandate of the Soviet Constitution to foster anti-religious propaganda. Maybe as a gesture to outraged critics, the response feebly commented that perhaps Kitchko "had not carried out his task in the best way." *Naie Presse* sharply rejected the Novosti statement and called for immediate withdrawal of the pamphlet and an investigation into its publication. M. Vilner, the editor of the paper, told the New York *Times:* "I have found as much indignation over the book in Communist circles as in Jewish circles . . . The only acceptable Soviet response would be an official investigation into the circumstances surrounding the publication, its suppression and punishment of those responsible for it."

As criticism continued to mount, Kremlin leaders backpedaled. On April 14, 1964, the day preceding the first Washington meeting of the American Jewish Conference on Soviet Jewry, the Ideological Commission of the Central Committee of the Communist Party published in *Pravda* a partial repudiation of the Kitchko book:

"The author of the book and the authors of the preface wrongly interpreted some questions concerning the emergence and development of this religion (Judaism)." The commission conceded that "a number of mistaken propositions and illustrations could insult the feelings of believers and might even be interpreted in the spirit of anti-Semitism." As an excuse the commission reminded everyone that a book merely serves as one tool in the nation's continued campaign against all religions, then added: "There is no such thing as anti-Semitism in the U.S.S.R. and cannot be."

Acknowledging this Kremlin concession, the leadership of the Jewish organizations assembled in Washington expressed gratification at the Communist Party pronouncement. They said, however, that the case showing existing Soviet anti-Semitism would be documented during their forthcoming meeting. They demanded that all contributors to the book be punished according to Soviet law and that the volume be withdrawn from circulation.

Other Anti-Semitic Literature

Sovietologists, though affronted by the crudeness of the Kitchko book, were not really surprised by it since the effort was consistent with a growing anti-Jewish Soviet campaign. Whether under the guise of anti-religious or anti-Israel material, propaganda attacks were being turned out freely and were suspected by many experts to be controlled and directed by the KGB.

One such volume, reissued in 1962 by Gospolitzdat, the Government Publishing House for Political Literature, was the eighteenth-century *A Gallery of Saints*, by Baron Holbach, printed in an edition of 175,000 copies. The book devotes fifty pages to anti-Semitic stereotypes describing Jews as being "always enemies of the human species" and claiming that they "prescribed cruelty, inhumanity, intolerance, thievery, treason, perfidy." The Holbach writings serve as a source book for Russia's atheistic writers and lecturers, although even *Jewish Cur-*

rents, the pro-Soviet publication in New York, expressed amazement in an article that such a book should be published today for general use. Even at the time of the Holbach piece, *Jewish Currents* said, "It was unphilosophical, crude, vehement and exaggerated in an age in which unbelievers had not yet ceased to be surprised at their own unbelief."

However, in 1963, a year before the Kitchko book, the Ideological Commission had endorsed another anti-Semitic exercise as "scientific standard." This was *Catechism Without Embellishment,* prepared by A. Osipov, a former priest and one of the U.S.S.R.'s most noted atheistic writers. The book lashes out viciously at Judaism, terming "God the principal bloodsucker where Jews are concerned." In another excerpt, it states:

The first thing we come across is the preaching of intolerance, the bloody extermination of people of other faiths, the land of which the Jews themselves prepared to seize . . . God recommends real racial discrimination to the Jews, the very same discrimination which is now branded and cursed by all the world's progressive people and nations. The very same discrimination for which the Jews paid such a high price in the days of Fascism when about seven million of them were exterminated. But in the Bible, God himself promises the Jews he'll cast out and destroy other nations, and advises them not to associate with nor become related to them and to outrage their religions.

This book received a far wider distribution than the limited edition of Kitchko, being produced by the Moscow State Publishing House for Political Literature in a Russian-language edition of 105,000 copies. At that time, outcries also reached the Kremlin, but the work was not withdrawn.

While some authorities consider the Osipov work far worse as an anti-Semitic display, the Kitchko book was more vehemently protested because of its outlandish cartoons. Meanwhile, the Kitchko apology turned out to be an isolated incident. Other material kept pouring off the presses, and about five months after the Soviet retreat on the Kitchko book, Label Katz, B'nai B'rith president, held up the latest Soviet tract at a press conference in New York. This was a ninety-six-page product of the Moldavian State Publishing House, *Contemporary Judaism and Zionism* by F. Mayatsky, replete with stock phrases and misstatements against the Jewish religion, Israel and Zionism. This book, published in February 1964, but unavailable in the West until much later, showered Judaism with such phrases as:

Judaism kills love of the Soviet motherland;

Judaism cripples the consciousness of people;

Judaism advocates contempt of labor and biological hatred of other peoples;

Jewish chauvinism gives rise to the Zionist theory of the "community of interests" of all Jews and even in the Soviet Union, Zionist agents succeed in recruiting people to go to Israel, the land of the fathers;

Judaism is a double-eyed reactionary ideology. It justifies the social injustice existing in the capitalistic world.

Katz told reporters the real dangers of the book were represented by its repeated charges against Judaism as an "international conspiracy," and other familiar charges bandied about at the height of Stalin's anti-Semitic campaign.

Paul Novick, the editor of the leftist *Morning Freiheit,* criticized the Mayatsky edition: ". . . the effect of the new booklet is not much better than that of the Kitchko booklets. Such books merely fortify anti-Semitism among the Soviet peoples."

Perhaps the best analysis was provided by Emanuel Litvinoff, editor of the quarterly, *Jews in Eastern Europe,* during a 1968 American lecture tour, when he said, "such tracts were written to nourish the prejudices of existing anti-Semites and to engender hatred of Jews among those still free of it. The U.S.S.R. today has become the leading producer of anti-Semitic material."

Perhaps the best proof that these campaigns receive official approval from the top comes in the shocking knowledge that Kitchko, after a brief hibernation, in 1968 received a high honor from the Supreme Soviet Ukrainian Communist Party on behalf of the Znanie Society.

Russia vehemently denies that there is anti-Semitism in the Soviet Union—certainly not as a policy—and is quick to point to its penal laws which provide punishment, and even exile, for attempts to sow racial or national hatred. "This law is strictly observed," according to Solomon Rabinovich, a writer for the Novosti Press Agency.

Current events, however, repeatedly give the lie to

such arrogant virtue, and the example of Kitchko is the best there is. Here is a racist of the most blatant vulgarity, who gains in virulence what he lacks in sophistication, and who is permitted (or perhaps encouraged) to operate without noticeable restriction, and even with reward. If the Soviet Union were sincere in its pretensions, the likes of Kitchko would never have seen a word of their writings in print.

IX

President Kennedy and the Soviet Jews

The material in the ensuing chapter is based largely on a lengthy and detailed confidential memorandum known even today only to a handful of American Jewish leaders.

The document was written by Philip Baum, international affairs director of the American Jewish Congress, after a meeting that Goldberg had with presidents of Jewish organizations and was intended to reach only a few top national figures.

The hope of American Jews for a *rapprochement* with the Russians reached its zenith during the administration of the late President John F. Kennedy, when three prominent Jews set into motion a dialogue at the highest level of government.

Arthur J. Goldberg, then Associate Justice of the Supreme Court, together with Senators Jacob K. Javits of New York and Abraham Ribicoff of Connecticut felt that perhaps the United States should officially broach the subject of discrimination against the Jews with the Soviet Union. The time had come, they felt, to end the silence in this matter, particularly among American Jews.

They called on Secretary of State Dean Rusk in Sep-

tember 1963, and found that the problem was familiar
to Rusk. However, he suggested that, rather than make
this a unilateral American approach, an international
committee of leading Jews should seek a meeting with
Soviet officials. The conferees, however, felt such a course
would lend support to the perennial Communist accusations that world Jewry was part of an international conspiracy. They left the meeting with an impression that
the Secretary of State was "sympathetic but cautious,"
which is the attitude of the State Department to this
day.

A few days later, Goldberg and Ribicoff, as former
cabinet members, were invited to the White House to
receive plaques in recognition of their services. According to Goldberg, they raised the subject of Soviet Jews
with the President, were surprised by his comprehensive
knowledge of the problem and learned that some months
previously, Kennedy had been approached on the same
question by his special counsel, Meyer Feldman. Feldman himself told me he was specifically concerned for
the Jews wishing to rejoin relatives from whom they had
been separated since World War II.

Before the Nazis invaded Russia, German and Red
armies divided conquered Poland. Thousands of Jewish
and non-Jewish families from Poland and other countries
sought escape routes. Frequently families were compelled
to separate, some fleeing to the West and others into
the Soviet Union. Immediately after World War II, an
opportunity was given to many of these families to re-
unite, but thousands were unable to take advantage of
this lapse in Soviet immigration regulations. Based on

recent Soviet figures, more than 50,000 families still remain separated.

Feldman said Kennedy was favorable to the emigration of Jews from the Soviet Union, but stated there was little he could do about it at the time except for sending personal messages to Khrushchev, or perhaps utilizing private diplomatic channels.

Then he offered to take the question up with Andrei Gromyko, the Soviet Foreign Minister, who had requested a meeting, and asked Feldman to prepare a memorandum. The document, prepared with the assistance of the State Department, was given to the President. But a Berlin Autobahn incident changed the meeting with Gromyko into a major discussion of East-West tensions, leaving no chance to use the document itself.

According to Feldman the President did raise the question of divided families and the larger problem of Soviet Jews, but Gromyko replied the Soviet Government could not publicly, or in any official way, respond to this overture. He did, however, assure Kennedy that the matter would be looked into "sympathetically."

Feldman said that while Kennedy believed Gromyko would inform Khrushchev, he held little hope anything would be done. Some time later when the aide inquired, Kennedy said he had not heard from Gromyko, but would talk to him again. Apparently he did, for shortly afterward the President told Feldman of a Soviet report that the best they could do at the present time "regarding the divide families" would be to temper the current prohibitions.

After the award ceremony, with Goldberg and Ribicoff in his office, Kennedy telephoned to discuss the matter with his chief adviser on Soviet affairs, Ambassador Llewellyn Thompson. Thompson, who only a few weeks earlier had told Label Katz, president of B'nai B'rith, that direct action on behalf of Soviet Jews would be "counterproductive," and suggested that the matter with the Soviets be pursued by a delegation of American businessmen going on an exchange visit. He thought this would be the most delicate way, but Goldberg and Ribicoff felt such an avenue was inappropriate. Instead, they suggested that, as a prelude to higher-level discussion with Khrushchev, a meeting be arranged with Soviet Ambassador Anatoly F. Dobrynin.

The Meeting with Dobrynin

The next morning Thompson telephoned Goldberg that the President had asked him to arrange an appointment for the delegation with Dobrynin. He said he had made it clear to Dobrynin that, while he was not seeking the meeting directly on behalf of the President, there was no doubt of Kennedy's personal interest. On October 29, 1963, Goldberg, Ribicoff and Javits met with Dobrynin and during a four-hour conversation examined the entire range of grievances regarding the Soviet's treatment of its more than three million Jews.

Dobrynin took violent exception to every point, particularly the statement that Jews were being singled out for prosecution in the then-current series of economic trials. He denied that discrimination existed in employment and education, and repeated the familiar Soviet line that Jews were employed in professions such as medicine, science, engineering and other technical crafts.

"We are proud of our Jewish citizens," the ambassador said. "They are treated like everyone else."

He startled the delegates by denying Jews were required to register as Jews when applying for internal passports or identification documents, claiming this was optional. He also expressed chagrin that the entire question had received so much prominence in the United States, saying that this could only hinder international harmony.

In response, the three explained that as individuals, privately and professionally, they were doing a great deal to improve relations between East and West, but felt that Soviet anti-Semitism was a real stumbling block on the road to improved relations. Not only Jews, but all men of good will shared their opinion, they added. At the end of the meeting they asked Dobrynin whether any positive purpose could be served by continuing their talks with Khrushchev in Moscow.

Dobrynin replied that the chairman had already been apprised of the meeting and would receive a full report. He would be the better judge whether further conversation could be helpful. If so, the leader's decision would be communicated to Goldberg. To this day there has been none, and Dobrynin never again referred to the conference.

The Presidents' Conference

At about this time Goldberg requested an urgent meeting of a group known as the Conference of Presidents of Major American Jewish Organizations. This is an advisory board representing twenty-one major American Jewish secular and religious agencies. On November 19, 1963, when the group met, Goldberg and Javits reported on their conference with Dobrynin.

Goldberg said that while the confrontation served the purpose of once again impressing upon the Soviet Union this country's deepening concern, he felt the ambassador's ineffective answers demanded a change of course on the part of the Jewish community from quiet diplomacy to responsible public protest.

The impression carried away from the meeting was that the Russians were becoming testy about the issue and still counted on what they felt was divisiveness within the American Jewish community to prevent united Jewish action.

Goldberg cautioned, however, that protest must never be imprudent. Protests to the U. S. Government must never be linked to any direct relationship between the United States and the Soviet Union. The question of the Jews in the U.S.S.R. should always be kept on a humanitarian plane, above political consideration. These objectives have been strictly adhered to since then by the organized Jewish community.

Goldberg also proposed that Jewish organizations mount a nationwide educational campaign to familiarize everyone with the problem and encouraged plans for a mobilization conference in the spring of 1964, calling together a broad representation from national Jewish agencies and individual communities. Meanwhile, Goldberg said that he, Javits and Ribicoff, would pursue the desired meeting with Khrushchev as well as possible other action by President Kennedy, a course that was aborted by history.

The Jewish leaders left the Washington meeting optimistic and heartened. Kennedy's understanding of, and sensitivity to most Jewish issues was well known, and because of this, his statements and assertions inspired confidence. The conferees sensed not only an imminent easing of tensions between East and West, but that the Soviets would not permit a peripheral issue, such as that of the Jews, to hinder a *rapprochement*.

Three days later, an assassin's bullet robbed the country of its leader and the Jewish community of one of its staunchest and most powerful friends.

X

Further Attempts to Organize

Organized Jewry was nevertheless aroused, and a year later, in 1964, nearly five hundred Jewish leaders convened in an unprecedented series of meetings for two days at the Willard Hotel, Washington, D.C.

The purpose was not merely to register protest, not only to educate the Jewish individual and enlist his support, not alone to lay the problem before the bar of world opinion, but to try and persuade President Johnson and the State Department to bring something of their enormous influence to bear on a dilemma that seemed destined for disaster.

The involvement of our government was not without precedent. In 1840, the United States protested the arrest and torture of Jews in Damascus, who were charged with the familiar blood-libel. In 1866, the government moved to cancel a discriminatory clause against Jewish emigration from a treaty with Switzerland. In 1913, after more than thirty years of outcry against Russian pogroms, Washington nullified a mutual travel and commercial treaty with Russia.

In 1964, the conferees adopted an eighteen-point manifesto which they hoped would elicit presidential support. They knew Johnson had been briefed, but also that he lacked Kennedy's intuitive understanding of Jewish problems.

A delegation finally obtained an invitation to the White House, where they talked with McGeorge Bundy and Lee White, aides to the President, and with George Reedy, the press secretary.

Lewis Weinstein of Boston, chairman of the conference and spokesman for the delegation, explained that silence could no longer be tolerated, even with the threat of Russian reprisals, and outlined steps the government could consider.

Bundy ruefully described past frustrations, in particular a conversation with Soviet Ambassador Dobrynin who had declared: "We have no problems with our Jewish citizens," to which Bundy replied: "Well, whatever it is you have no problem about, we're having a lot of protests on!"

President Johnson entered the room at this point and greeted everyone personally. Bundy summarized the preceding conversation, and the President reviewed his own human rights record and sympathy for the state of Israel. He promised to discuss the matter with Secretary of State Dean Rusk the following morning.

Some time before, Johnson had talked about Russian Jews with Meyer Feldman, the former White House counsel, who commented: "As vice-president he was not involved, but when he became President we did have some discussions, very early, about Soviet Jewish policy regarding the Jewish population."

Feldman drafted a presidential message to a Jewish meeting in which Johnson unequivocally felt the Soviet

Government should permit Jews to emigrate. Feldman recalled that the President was aware of the facts, that he was sympathetic to the problem and that he would do what he could—although he felt there was little that could be done.

The following day the delegation met with Rusk and formally requested the State Department to convey the views of the conference to the Soviet Government. It was made quite clear that politics played no part in this, nor was there any intention to exacerbate the differences between the nations.

In the meantime, community meetings were held throughout the nation; state and local governments were urged to adopt resolutions, and citizens from all walks of life were oriented to the issue and called upon to participate actively in the growing tide of protest.

On October 28, 1964, shortly before the presidential election, Johnson sent a message to ten thousand protesters at Madison Square Garden, New York, in which he voiced deep and continued concern over the plight of Soviet Jews and stated: "The Administration will continue to search for practical methods of alleviating (their) position." He encouraged similar rallies and concomitant actions, since any official move would be meaningless "unless reinforced by the pressures of an aroused world public opinion."

This represented what may have been the high point of the President's involvement, since a year later, on September 19, 1965, his message to another 10,000 men, women and children conducting a vigil opposite the White House contained little more than recognition of the facts of U.S.S.R. life. An attempt to meet with him failed, and vigil leaders had to content themselves with another friendly talk with White House aides, who offered good will and the by-then familiar "Its a delicate matter, and we'll continue to do whatever we can."

The vigil, however, excited the imaginations of millions and received widespread publicity throughout the world.

Addressing the demonstrators, James Roosevelt, U.S. representative to the United Nations Economic Council, cried out: "The Soviet Union intends to atomize the Jewish community, to estrange it from its past, to pulverize its identity, to crush its historical consciousness, to destroy every possibility of Jewish group survival!"

Roosevelt insisted that the race issue in this country was not analagous to Russian treatment of the Jews. "Here the Negro has the right to take the fight into his own hands," he said, "and public opinion has helped his cause."

Bayard Rustin, the Negro leader, drew cheers when he said: "I would like to see the Soviet Union permit the kind of non-violent demonstrations being carried out across this nation. We who have suffered oppression for three hundred and fifty years know what it is to face the sort of pressures exerted by the Soviet Government on its Jewish citizens."

Many Negro leaders subsequently supported the Jewish effort. The late Dr. Martin Luther King, Jr. participated at many rallies and meetings, voicing the plea: "You must not relent until the religious and cultural deprivations of three million Soviet Jews are completely exposed and conditions changed."

After the vigil, a considerable number of demonstrators bearing petitions signed by more than one million Americans, left the White House and walked quietly to the Soviet embassy. At the door, four men stood together in a symbol of unity. They were Theodore Bikel, the actor-folksinger who is a vice-president of the American Jewish Congress; Rabbi Seymour Cohen of Chicago, AJCSJ chairman; Rev. John Cronin of the National Catholic Welfare Conference, and Rustin. They rang the doorbell repeatedly. The embassy remained mute and shuttered. Bikel thrust a single petition under the door, and the vigil came to an end.

The ensuing months were active ones for the American Jewish Conference on Soviet Jewry. Even at a ceremony in Montreal, marking the inauguration of a Canada-Russia passenger-ship link, Rabbi Harry Stern of Temple Emanu-El, Montreal, went aboard the S.S. *Pushkin* to hand the captain a message calling attention to the great moral problem.

Patrick Cardinal O'Boyle of Washington called upon Christians to "raise their voices loud and strong against this inhuman tyranny of man against man." John C. Bennett, the Protestant theologian, declared: "Christians have a special responsibility to work by public protest, and by any means available to them, for ending of these anti-Semitic policies and practices by the Soviet Union."

Perhaps the most moving reaction came during the U.S.S.R.'s fiftieth anniversary year, when more than 150,000 religious-school children collected nickels and dimes to pay for three full-page advertisements in the New York *Times* asking of Premier Kosygin, in essence:

"Is it a happy anniversary for more than three million Russians of Jewish faith who are not permitted to have one Jewish school?"

The Department of State—a Stumbling Block

Most of the time, in matters relating to foreign policy, members of the executive branch defer to the judgment of the State Department. The American Jewish leadership has always cast a suspicious eye on the old-guard "Waspish" make-up of the State Department. Too frequently the views of the viciously anti-Zionist American Council for Judaism are warmly received by some members of the Department since these views coincide with diplomatic recognition of Arab interests. Regarding Israel, many career officers believe the U.S. must cater more to 100 million Arabs than to 2.5 million Jews. Some Jewish spokesmen concur with Arthur Morse's indictment, charging that during World War II, State Department officials "failed to use the governmental machinery at their disposal to rescue Jews from Hitler." The author of *While Six Million Died* documented in his book how the Department even used government machinery to prevent the rescue of these Jews during the war.

Political ambivalence, which often attains the level of fine art, is epitomized in the State Department by public pronouncements widely at variance with private statements. In one flurry of viewpoints exchanged recently, a public statement was made at the State Department that "we" (presumably the State Department) strongly disapproved of the Soviet Government's pressures on the

Jews. Off the record, the private viewpoint of some officials was that American Jewish complaints against the U.S.S.R. were "hysterical."

Jewish leaders, though wary still, no longer regard the State Department today as "the big bad wolf." Jehuda Hellman, executive director of the Presidents' Conference, believes that the Department has been friendly, if cautious, toward the Jewish community since World War II, "providing information, briefings, assessments, and aiding us in many situations."

"I think State Department officials have concluded that bigots who promulgate anti-Semitism in other countries are the same who work contrary to American interests. Because of inherent caution, however, the State Department will not stick its neck out for the Jewish community. They don't want to be the knight in shining armor, and therefore will encourage Jews to seek others to apply pressure."

The State Department also prefers that others assume leadership in the United Nations, where the Human Rights Committee and Social and Humanitarian Committee also serve as forums.

Although these debates provide hardly more than a moral force and a pulse of opinion, they are nonetheless observed by international representatives and a large press corps. The U.S.S.R.'s reaction ranges from caustic replies to outright aggressiveness. Over a two-year period (1965–67) the Russians were successful in removing any reference to anti-Semitism, in a proposed declaration on human rights, by equating anti-Semitism with Nazism and Zionism.

Nowhere is the State Department's changing attitudes better exemplified than in statements by Mrs. Marietta Tree, chief U.S. delegate to the UN Human Rights Commission, and by Morris Abram, who served several years in the same capacity.

At the UN on March 11, 1964, Mrs. Tree said: anti-Semitism constitutes "a danger in the past and a danger today. . . . We must recognize that some states where laws forbid discrimination in the most forceful terms nevertheless carry on policies which are designed to have the effect of obliterating an ethnic group . . . (through the) deprivation of the religious and cultural heritage which make this group unique."

At no point in her 1300 word statement did Mrs. Tree make any reference to the Soviet Union's discrimination against its Jews.

Five years later, Abram officially stated:

The U.S.S.R. engages in the vicious cartooning and harpooning of Jews . . . replaying the anti-Semitic Tsarist and Nazi themes of conspiracy.

The policy of the Department also changed regarding public protests and declarations by Congress. A resolution introduced by Senator Ribicoff in 1964 received watered-down treatment in the Senate Foreign Relations Committee following State Department pressure.

In the early days of the protest movement, Leslie H. Whitten, a writer for the Hearst newspapers, similarly found little interest on the part of State Department officials in protest notes or public pronouncements. However, on the day after the Washington Vigil, State Department Public Affairs officer William Stearman told a delegation briefing: "This sort of public demonstration is the best way to help arouse public opinion around the world and the best way to help Soviet Jewry."

An official information bulletin described and acknowledged the harsh restrictions against Soviet Jews, but doubted the government's capability to take direct action. "We have found from past experience that the government-to-government approach to Soviet officials at all levels is totally ineffective. While official government actions can be dismissed by Soviet authorities as propaganda, the expressions of concern by large numbers of private individuals are more difficult to ignore. We see no real indication yet that the Soviet Government is willing to make the significant concessions which would be required to enable Jewish life in the Soviet Union to flourish as it has in that part of the world in past centuries, or even to restore the Jewish educational, cultural and religious institutions which existed before 1948."[1]

In my discussions with high-ranking State Department Sovietologists and authorities on Eastern Europe, a friendly attitude prevailed—although during periods of East-West tensions, I was told that any direct representation by the U. S. Government becomes ineffective. The experts feel that protests have greater meaning when they come from impartial and less passionate sources such as Latin America and non-NATO nations. In their opinion, if enough of them make personal contacts to the Soviet Union, eventually the Russians would have to relax their restrictions against the Jews.

One individual mentioned that the Jewish situation is

discussed at Department briefings and said the Department would provide specific information to any group seeking data on the Jewish question. While effective, this method presents a basic built-in danger, since only keen observers of the Soviet scene are able to counter Soviet propaganda responses. On the other hand, repeated raising of the issue cannot help but keep the Russians alert and produce minor gains for Soviet Jews.

Privately, such representation has been made, and voices were raised by a number of nations. Off-the-record discussions about Soviet Jews were held by Belgium's Paul Henri Spaak and the former French Premier, Pierre Mendès-France. Another conversation took place between Canada's Paul Martin, Secretary of State for External Affairs, and Kremlin leaders during his visit to Moscow in March 1967. Perhaps with one eye on badly needed Canadian wheat, Soviet officials did not dismiss the question with the typical, "It's an internal problem," or "We have none," excuse. Instead, they told the Canadian minister that steps were being taken to remedy the situation.

As far as American influence with the Soviet Union is concerned, Meyer Feldman says: "The long view of history is that the United States and the Soviet Union must work together. Otherwise both die."

Curious about differences that may have existed between President Kennedy and President Johnson on the handling of this issue, I remarked: "I have the impression that Mr. Johnson, while sympathetic, was not willing to move quite so quickly as Mr. Kennedy." Feldman replied: "I believe that President Kennedy would have continued to pursue contacts outside normal diplomatic lines in an effort to obtain some result. I don't think Kennedy would have been any more effective than Johnson, because of the relationship between the Soviet Union and the United States, but I think his idea was to grasp an opportunity and, hopefully, get some commitment."

A high-ranking member of the Department took a look into the future. "If circumstances arose and the President met with either Kosygin or Brezhnev," he said, "we would urge him to open discussions on the subject. Barring such a meeting, representation could be made on the foreign ministry level."

While sympathetic to the reasons put forth for limited contacts on a presidential level, Jewish leaders here during this period assumed that their constant pressure resulted in American ambassadors raising the question at the Kremlin. No substantive corroboration was forthcoming, although in 1959, Llewellyn Thompson during his first tour as ambassador to Moscow saw to it that about one hundred Yiddish books and periodicals were included in an American book exhibition in the U.S.S.R. Thompson was reluctant to take more direct action and later advised Kennedy to have businessmen raise the issue with Soviet leaders. I was told at the State Department that Ambassador Foy D. Kohler never spoke about the Jewish issue to anyone in the Soviet upper echelon, either, but confined his discussions to Soviet intellectuals at social functions.

Stephen S. Rosenfeld, Washington *Post* editorial writer, wrote that he had been told in 1964 that "Further efforts could be construed as interference in Soviet domestic affairs. They would only tempt continued Soviet criticism of America's racial problems and lend credence to the Russian accusation that Jews are agents of a foreign power."

The Protests of Friends

While Russia is sensitive to international opinion, the most telling effect upon the Kremlin is made by neutral, or Socialist and Communist sources. The Kitchko incident demonstrated how quickly Moscow responded when Western Communist parties repudiated anti-Semitism.

One noted critic has been the Italian Communist Party, whose members were confused, assuming anti-Semitism to be incompatible with Communist philosophy, and who believed that Roman Catholicism lay at the foundation of this social evil.

In 1966, a volume of essays, *The Jews in the U.S.S.R.*, by leading English, Israeli and Italian experts, was published, analyzing the background and status of the problem. The preface, by Senator Umberto Terracini, a founder of the Italian Communist Party, stated: "It is difficult to see a valid explanation for the discriminatory policies still being carried out in the Soviet Union in regard to Jews, no matter what name is used to designate these policies."[2]

Publication of a proposed draft on "The Jewish Question" in the American Communist Party's publication, *Political Affairs*, in August 1966, brought to the surface in this country a harsh conflict between opposing factions within the party. Some considered assimilation a natural and inevitable process, especially under Communism; others envisioned the reality of a Jewish community and a Jewish culture even within the Soviet Union.

The principal defender of the latter viewpoint for more than a decade has been the New York City Communist Yiddish daily, *Morning Freiheit*. The newspaper frequently criticizes the Soviet Union for its policy of forced assimilation against Jews. Paul Novick, the editor, believes the U.S.S.R. is still carrying on a Stalinist holdover campaign of Russification and considers this contrary to Marxist teaching. While he lauds the small cultural gains, he charges that they are meager compared to the needs.

In sharp difference is Hyman Lumer, editor of *Political Affairs*, who challenges those who cite a decline of spoken Yiddish among Jews in the U.S.S.R. as evidence to prove the existence of a policy of assimilation. "Even when Yiddish was in its heyday, there were millions of Jews who did not speak Yiddish," he said. "It is true that the use of Yiddish is diminishing. The language of the majority of American Jews is English, but by this fact they do not cease to be Jews. In fact, there is more nationalism among English-speaking Jews, among whom Zionists and other nationalists hold sway, than among Yiddish-speaking adherents to the Yiddish classicists." (Correct, but then in the United States abundant cultural materials are available in English, as in the languages of other Western countries.)

C. Kenig, the French Communist editor of the Paris *Naie Presse*, reported on December 17, 1966, that among young and old Jews in the U.S.S.R. there were strong national sentiments. As with other observers, he found a great interest in the Yiddish theater and in Yiddish writing. He said that if this work was co-ordinated and greater effort was made to raise the quality and expand publicity, this would have a first-class cultural and educational significance for hundreds of thousands of Soviet Jews.

Whether friend or foe, Communist or capitalist, religious leader or businessman, or statesman on the right, left or in the middle, all of them, even though they may differ on the degree of discrimination, call for a drastic change in Soviet Jewish policy.

The Kosygin Promise on Divided Families

When Kosygin came to Great Britain in February 1967, he was greeted by an avalanche of protests against the U.S.S.R.'s anti-Jewish policies. Leading the way were 252 Conservative and Labor members of the House of Commons, expressing their concern in a resolution. The M.P.s enumerated their grievances in a letter to Kosygin and pressed the government of Prime Minister Harold Wilson to take the matter up with the Soviet visitor.

An educated and aroused British public, led by the Jewish community, exerted enormous pressure with letters to newspapers, protest meetings, special religious services and a march by 2200 students, communal leaders, rabbis and priests. They carried placards in front of the U.S.S.R. embassy and made an attempt to see Kosygin (he ignored them).

The London *Times* asked: "What about your promise,

a few months ago, about divided families from World War II now being allowed to emigrate?"

The reference was to a statement made on December 3, 1966, at a Paris press conference, where in response to a question about dispersed Jewish families Kosygin said: "As far as the reunification of families is concerned, the road is open to families who wish to meet or wish to leave the Soviet Union, and there is no problem about it."[3]

The statement created cautious optimism throughout the world. The American embassy in Moscow inquired whether the Premier's statement meant any change in Soviet emigration policies. The reply, as released by the State Department to the author, made these points: that the Soviet Union was re-examining its emigration policies; that local authorities decided whether exit visas could be granted; that there were twice as many émigrés in 1966 as in 1965, and that although they were not "throwing open the door," emigration would increase gradually of its own accord. Indeed, in 1967, 151 Jewish immigrants and visitors did come to the United States, compared to 96 the year before (see table).

A much larger exodus occurred to Israel. When the U.S.S.R. broke off diplomatic relations at the outset of the Arab-Israel conflict, nearly two hundred families were prevented from emigrating. They had received permission from Soviet authorities and visas from the Netherlands embassy, handling Israel's diplomatic affairs, and had been granted permission to leave.

In a defensive speech before the UN Human Rights Committee, U.S.S.R. delegate Evgeny Nasinovsky asked,

EMIGRATION FIGURES

Soviet Exit Visas Received by U. S. Embassy, Moscow

Year	Immigrants	Estimated Jewish	Private Visitors	Estimated Jewish
1961	114	6	11	2
1962	129	5	2	0
1963	128	10	10	2
1964	133	15	28	5
1965	287	35	176	50
1966	298	16	477	80
1967	266	51	799	110
1968	205	53	500*	170

* Does not include September–December figures.

"Why must this question be raised everywhere? And trumpeted about? And, mostly, they (the *émigrés*) even come back! If a Russian Jew did go to Israel, he is an atheist and forced to be religious. Otherwise they don't even give him citizenship." (A lie, since all Jews may become Israeli citizens based upon the "Law of Return" automatically granting them this right.)

The question of divided families was always uncomfortable for the Russians, since their plight has won the hearts of many outstanding world figures and statesmen. A consistent champion of the Soviet Jewish cause, British Premier Wilson held discussions in June 1963, with Khrushchev, Gromyko and others about Soviet Jewish policy, particularly the question of divided families in Western countries and Israel. British Socialist leaders Hugh Gaitskell and Aneurin Bevan had discussed the matter with the Russians in 1959, as had Wilson on an earlier journey.

At the 1963 meeting, Khrushchev showed great eagerness to please the Labor Party delegation, because he needed help in securing new British-Soviet trade agreements. According to reliable sources, Wilson told Khrushchev, "How can we recommend that our government deal with you when you are barbarians?" Startled, the Russian inquired why Wilson thought they were barbarians. Wilson pulled out a list containing the names of seven persons separated from their families since the Nazi holocaust. Khrushchev sought immediately to rectify the grievance and instructed Gromyko to look into the matter. Four months later, the first of the seven separatees reached London.

Soviet roadblocks toward large-scale emigration, however, were evident soon after the Kosygin promise in Paris. Believing they saw a green light at last, many Jewish families in the U.S.S.R., whose requests to emigrate had previously been turned down, flocked to Soviet passport offices holding copies of *Izvestia* and *Pravda*. (Applicants thus risk exposure. Cases have been reported where persons found themselves demoted or expelled from universities when authorities learned they wished to emigrate. Cases are also known where children had been made to vow before their classmates that they would refuse to accompany their parents if the latter were to leave the Soviet Union.[4] Everywhere the authorities blocked efforts by Jews who sought applications. Articles were published questioning the loyalty of citizens contemplating departure from the motherland and describing widespread unemployment in Israel.

Though our visit occurred prior to the Kosygin promise, the anxieties and emotions of these divided families were brought home to me dramatically. Someone brushed past me in the crowded sanctuary of a synagogue after the service. Back at my hotel, I reached into my pocket and found a handwritten letter addressed to the UN Human Rights Committee. Judging from the worn envelope and the faded ink, the letter had obviously been sitting in a coat pocket for a long time waiting for the right carrier. It was written in English by the son of a family of five, who was anxious to join his family in Israel. I presented the letter, in New York, to the Human Rights Committe, via the American representative, Morris Abram.

It follows:

Gentlemen:

The situation which is going to be disclosed before you is not one of disaster. Neither is it one of evil forces at work. It rather would be safely described as an entirely abnormal for any civilized community, and as such disgraceful.

We are Jews and what we want is to be let out and come to Israel of course.

My family consists of father, mother, me, my brother and my wife.

My mother's and father's families had left Russia in 1920–21 fleeing from pogroms and starvation, my parents being at the time of a preschool age. For about ten years they lived and were educated in Palestine, then a country under the British mandate. Unfortunately, they came to be subject to Communist influences and after a period of persecution including imprisonment they both were deported in 1930 to the country of their origin.

The deportation was considered lawful by the British authorities for neither of the young saboteurs "had a British citizenship," a too costly thing and really a luxury for the dwellers of Palestine. I should emphasize the unwillingness of the deported and for the brutality of the forced division of relatives.

Four sisters and a brother have been living since then in Israel. My mother's parents both have died there without her being able to attend their deathbeds. The senior brother of my father has also been living there all these years.

I believe you are acquainted enough with the life in this country to be able to understand why for thirty-five years my parents haven't found a chance to get back. I, personally, can't blame them for that. Since those were the years of THE FEAR, and in greater part the years of persecution. My parents were not only Jews which is a serious enough crime in itself, they had and still have an extraordinarily strange biography, and one's biography is a very important thing here. Besides they were acknowledged friends of the "people's enemies," that is, political refugees from Palestine who were almost all jailed and the majority murdered.

Moreover, I am proud of them for they haven't lost contact with our relatives through correspondence however hard the time was and they haven't given up their belief in good and in our future.

Last year as late as it was we began to do something about this. I won't introduce you to many particular details and say only there was a lot of humiliation. My wife and my brother happened to study at one Institute here in (name of city). It is an Institute for the study of metals. They both were witch-hunted out of Komsomol and subsequently formally excluded from the Institute, "for the behavior unworthy of the Soviet student." Their crime is their wish to go to Israel with their closest relatives. I can only add to this that my wife was about to defend her diploma after six years study, the date fixed, and my brother was finishing his fourth year of study. Now he is bound to be conscripted.

We were able to collect all the necessary documents and

characteristics and to present a petition to the Soviet Government asking for permission to go to Israel with an object of
uniting our family and returning from exile. We were refused
and no reasons named. Separate petitions to the Prime Minister and to the Party leader with the detailed description of
our case failed to produce any answer.

Allow me to assure you that we, all of us, are firmly set
upon our decision. And nothing can change our attitude.
Our long wished for aim can be achieved, but when? And
what can change their attitude?

I am convinced, gentlemen, it is you who have the answer.
So I am asking for your HELP.

With great respect
signature

Although the question of divided families is still un-
settled and no clear-cut directives exist, a trickle of emigration to Israel and the West is permitted. According to
the November 24, 1969 issue of *Newsweek,* prior to 1967,
two hundred Jews emigrated every month to Israel. Exit
permits were stopped for eighteen months after the war
and resumed in January 1969 to the current rate of 275
per month. The magazine stated that 80,000 Russian Jews
have filled out applications for exit visas. One does not
know on what basis Russian citizens who want to leave
the country are granted visas to do so, but an unwritten
basis does exist.

At the same time, there are cases on record where
Russian Jews have been jailed or severely punished
merely for requesting permission to leave. The Russian
bureaucratic mind is unfathomable in this respect.

CONCLUSION

Where Do We Go from Here?

Understanding the misfortune of the modern Russian Jew can only be achieved when one also understands three premises acknowledged by most Sovietologists.

One is that official anti-Semitism is unlikely to diminish to any marked extent in the foreseeable future. There are, of course, intellectual circles in the Soviet Union where the tiny flame of knowledge burns brightly, if secretly, and among Russian Jews themselves oppression serves to polarize the mystic and seminal ties with the ethics of their forefathers.

The weight of anti-Semitism, however, is immovable at present. It can be expected to lessen periodically under the equal weight of world opinion or internal expediency (such as the employment of a Jewish cosmonaut—Lt. Col. Boris Volynov—whose antecedents are carefully hidden), or vanish when the Kremlin realizes that anti-Semitism destroys more than it accomplishes.

Rabbi Jacob J. Weinstein makes the point that anti-Semitism is "an anachronism which has a pernicious effect of casting doubt even on those features of Communism which right-thinking men must welcome as harbingers of social justice, which dreamers and thinkers have labored for over the centuries."

If the regime encourages economic, social and religious discrimination against one segment of its people, can other nationality groups rest easy? Dr. Weinstein wonders. And do Soviet leaders not realize that in the eyes of free men anti-Semitism "serves to divert attention from the really constructive developments that have taken place in Soviet Russia?"

Apparently not, for though anti-Semitism follows a predictable course of periodic remission, its demise in the U.S.S.R. is wishful thinking. Moreover, the "Jewish question," to use the Hitlerian phrase, is intimately associated with the state of Israel.

In the days immediately after the establishment of the State of Israel, relations between the two countries were cordial, and the pressures against the Jew in Russia appeared slightly improved. When the honeymoon came to an end, it ended in both places. Today the leadership keeps anti-Semitism alive in its own precincts for many interlocking reasons, some only dimly perceived, and then against the background of neo-Leninism.

The Kremlin leaders, masters at the game of chess, hold three million pawns, which they use with cold and practical application to gain their ends in the Middle East and at home. Except, perhaps, for the intelligentsia, Russians accept dogma for reasons of personal security or as a safety valve. Thus, closing another synagogue, arresting another dozen Jews as scapegoats, staging another economic trial, are part of a plan which if not so specific as a blueprint, is still taken regularly from the shelf, dusted off and put into execution. From the Soviet point of view it is a good plan since it has never failed.

The second premise is that though the men at the top will change, their Jewish policies will not. The Marx-Lenin-Stalin syndrome is here to stay. Just as with the United States Government, so does the Soviet Union have checks and balances. Its system, however, is geared not to preserving freedom, but bondage of the soul, spirit, psyche, mind and body in order to achieve the devastation of capitalism and the victory of Communism.

In the New York *Times* of August 10, 1969, Henry Kamm, returning after two years in Moscow as correspondent of the newspaper, wrote: "The typical Soviet Jew feels, like other citizens, deprived of his human rights, only more so. He knows he lives in a country that is as anti-Semitic as the rest of Eastern Europe. But he is not outraged. He knows his place. He hopes that he will be left alone, if he keeps quiet, and his brothers abroad do the same. And who knows, perhaps, if he is allowed to live in peace, some day a leader will come along who will not require a Jew to be twice as good as all the other candidates to get the job."

Certainly not all Jews are as quiescent. On November 10, 1969, Israeli Premier Golda Meir made public "a heartfelt cry of distress" from eighteen Georgian Jewish families to the UN Human Rights Commission, pleading for the right to emigrate to Israel. Despite direct pressure from Soviet officials, the Georgian Jews refused to withdraw their appeals. A month later, a similar urgent request came signed by twenty-five Jews from Moscow.

The third premise has to do with the passion and contradiction of the Russian mind and its enormous, collective, underlying, terrorizing guilt. One refers now to the leadership.

In December 1968, Boris L. Kochubiyevsky, a thirty-year-old Jewish engineer from Kiev, was arrested and imprisoned on charges of slander after he applied for emigration to Israel. Prior to his arrest, but following a raid on his apartment, Kochubiyevsky appealed by letter to Communist Party chief Leonid Brezhnev to be permitted to seek his freedom.

The letter, which was smuggled out of the country, is heartbreaking and eloquent and probably tipped the scales against Kochubiyevsky. Yet, in May 1968, Yakow Kazakov, a twenty-one-year-old Moscow engineering student, wrote a similar letter to the Supreme Soviet and no punitive action was taken. Why?

In the Kremlin's unceasing assault upon Judaism in any form, some Jews are arrested on trumped-up charges, tried in court and castigated in one of several ways: some are deprived of their livelihoods and status or impeded in achieving a higher education, and yet some are elevated to positions of trust and confidence (especially in the sciences where they are needed) and others are permitted to emigrate. Why?

Why, for example, was Rabbi Yehuda Leib Levin of Moscow sent to visit this country in June 1968, to extol the virtues of life in the Soviet Union? Why was Nehama Lifschitz, the Lithuanian-born Russian folksinger, permitted to emigrate with her family to Israel in 1969, when her entire adult career had revolved around the symbolism she represented in reawakening identification among her massive audiences with Yiddish culture and a *raison d'être?*

Undoubtedly such incidents are a response to world opinion, but there was a time when such threats to "national security" would merely have been liquidated. Why are these concessions now made, if not for a disturbing complex of guilt perhaps spurred by sensitivity? That the Russians are inordinately sensitive about the Jews is a recognized fact. There is a somewhat greater availability of matzos at Passover. *Sovietisch Heimland* is still being printed, and has improved in content. Except for an isolated incident, there have been no further economic trials at this writing. The government has been cautious about the exercise of its internal policies relating to Jews and has taken pains to avoid anything like the Kitchko episode.

The international protest movement is largely responsible, but inside the country, Jews themselves have given signs of resistance in the only ways open to them. They now attend services, and congregate in the only places they may—the sixty-two remaining synagogues in the U.S.S.R. They attend every public performance remotely allied to Jewish content. At great personal risk, they seek out foreign Jewish visitors to speak with them and write letters to the Western world. They refuse to sign statements that attack Israel. They listen to recordings of Jewish origin and attempt to have their children learn Yiddish. To do more would be to risk reprisals against themselves and the entire remnant of Soviet Jewry, for at this stage the hierarchy cannot be pushed too hard. The

1969 invasion of Czechoslovakia was a case in point of the Russians reacting to change with hard suppression prompted by fear of change.

Yet, protest appears to be the only present effective course of action. Leonid Vladimirov, the Russian-Jewish author of *The Russians* (published in the United States in 1968, though the author defected to the West some time earlier), wrote: "I am absolutely positive that the effectiveness of the world protest movement about the plight of Soviet Jewry is great. It is actually now the only restricting force affecting the Kremlin's wild anti-Semites. So far as the future of Soviet Jews is concerned, I know only one thing which will never occur, and this is assimilation."

Counterpropaganda on a comprehensive scale is as much a part of Russian diplomacy as propaganda itself. Western leaders and the press are besieged by Soviet documents, releases, statements, magazines and assorted testaments which seek to prove that there is no Jewish problem. Russian diplomats, as part of their assignments, are in the vanguard of the official apologists and occasionally go to extreme, and even unethical, lengths to achieve their aims.

Few people know that in March 1965, Anatoli G. Mishkov, first secretary of the Soviet embassy in Washington, called upon Senator Abraham Ribicoff of Connecticut to persuade Ribicoff to withdraw a pending Senate resolution condemning anti-Semitism in the U.S.S.R.

Failing to impress an already aroused Ribicoff, the embassy dispatched a representative to the State Department to protest "attempts to interfere in the domestic affairs of the U.S.S.R." The irony was apparently lost on the embassy.

A year before, after the State Department had objected, a similar Senate resolution ended up as a simple declaration of human rights. This time, State did not interfere, and the strongly worded resolution was passed in the Senate unanimously on May 16, 1965.

Since to obtain a commitment from the State Department on a delicate and controversial matter is well-nigh impossible, American Jewish leaders have sought aid from successive presidents.

Soon after Mr. Nixon became President, the inquiry was made whether he would be willing to discuss the plight of Russian Jews at the summit level and whether he would encourage and endorse a meeting such as the one President Kennedy had arranged.

According to a report by Rabbi Herschel Schachter, Mr. Nixon, prior to his election, told the Presidents' Conference of Major American Jewish Organizations, that it was "important to create world opinion, as well as document all the facts, in order that through diplomatic and other channels the concern of the American people for the cultural and religious freedom of Soviet Jews may be firmly communicated on many levels to the leaders of the Soviet Government."

The key word is "diplomatic." The future President seemed to imply the use of American diplomacy, an implication that must have gladdened the members of the conference. A few months later, however, the emphasis had shifted subtly. An inquiry by the author to Ronald

L. Ziegler, press secretary to the President, elicited this reply:

"I am sure you understand why it is not possible to predict at this time what, precisely, might be discussed at a high-level meeting with Soviet leaders. On the general question of helping to improve the lot of Jews living in another country, the problem is not one of desire to help but of what are most appropriate and effective tactics for the U. S. Government."

Ziegler continued that the President had always considered non-official contacts to be an effective means of impressing other governments with the feelings of the American people. In the letter, Ziegler stated that President Nixon would endorse a delegation of Jewish leaders visiting Moscow to discuss the problem with Kremlin officials, such as the group that met with Soviet Ambassador Dobrynin (Goldberg, Javits and Ribicoff) sanctioned by the late President John F. Kennedy. What was being suggested was that if the Jews of this country were interested in the fate of their coreligionists they would do well to provide the help themselves.

While it is true that Israel and the Middle East are of paramount importance to Jews everywhere today, it is no less pressing, albeit on another level, that three million Jews in the Soviet Union are being systematically assimilatated. One wonders whether genocide of the spirit is more, or less, grave than destruction of the body.

The climate of friendly and diplomatic intervention may improve, but in the final analysis, the Jews of the free world must act as the collective messiah for their brethren. The President and the State Department must never be permitted to forget that the three million stand as a momentous and consequential priority in the minds of American Jews and that the government's friendship for Israel does not discharge the responsibility of men of good will toward those who are oppressed.

If the United States can be moved, other nations would quickly follow in applying moral pressure on Soviet leaders. If a Harold Wilson can continually champion the cause of Soviet Jews, even when international diplomacy suggests otherwise, why, then, can't the President of the bastion of "democratic freedoms" assume similar leadership?

Jewish organizations must intensify individual programs of education and selflessly provide the American conference on Soviet Jewry with an adequate annual budget and full-time professional staff, to deal with the Russian Jewish problem solely.

The finest public relations minds in the world should be engaged to blueprint a program of education, a liaison network with organizational overtones with constituted groups in other countries; also a detailed plan for exerting proper, but maximum, influence on governments throughout the world must be mobilized.

The concerned Jew who visits the Soviet Union cannot escape the fact of his ambassadorship without portfolio. The weight of history will have thrust the role upon him. The Jew who travels intellectually unprepared, morally righteous and interested primarily in Russian culture and caviar, will encounter no Jewish problem and probably no Jews. Jews who go to and support Israel should consider a visit to the Soviet Union equally as important.

The traveler who is canny and acute will overcome the difficulty of meeting Jews. He will talk to them in their homes, on the street, in the hidden park, in doorways. He will attend a religious service in a synagogue. He will closely observe the nuances of inflection and behavior that are peculiarly Jewish and cannot be bred out. He will learn much, and feel more, and be changed when he returns home to act and educate.

Senator Ribicoff aptly reminds us that history has demonstrated that "the silent onlooker becomes the moral accomplice to the crime." One only hopes that mankind will heed the impassioned plea of Soviet Jews:

"DO NOT FORGET US!"

FOOTNOTES

PREFACE

1. The White House, April 6, 1964.
2. New York *Times*, July 22, 1968.
3. *Commentary*, December 1963.
4. House Committee Report 174, May 10, 1965.
5. "Message of Israel," WABC Radio, September 12, 1965.

CHAPTER I

1. *The New York Times Magazine*, September 8, 1968.
2. *European Judaism*, Vol. 3, No. 1, Summer 1968.

CHAPTER II

1. *Jews of Silence*, Elie Wiesel, Holt, Rinehart & Winston, 1966, p. 65.

CHAPTER III

1. *The History of the Jews in Russia and Poland*, Simon Dubnov, Vol. II, p. 312, Jewish Publication Society, 1918.
2. *The Russian Jews Under the Tzars and Soviets*, p. 65, Salo W. Baron, Macmillan, 1964.
3. *The Jewish Problem in the Soviet Union*, B. Z. Goldberg, p. 353, Crown, 1961.
4. *Slavonic and East-European Review*, XL, pp. 155–56, Leonard Shapiro.

5. *History of the Jews in Russia and Poland*, Simon Dubnov, Vol. II, p. 56, Jewish Publication Society, 1918.
6. *The Kremlin, the Jews and the Middle East*, Judd L. Teller, p. 26, Thomas Yoseloff, 1957.
7. *The Jews in Russia*, Louis Greenberg, Vol. II, p. 158, Yale, 1951.
8. *The Jews in Russia*, Louis Greenberg, Vol. II, p. 159, Yale, 1951.
9. *The Jews in the Soviet Union*, Solomon Schwarz, p. 50, Syracuse University Press, 1951.
10. Ibid., p. 53.
11. Ibid., p. 53.
12. *Jews and the National Question*, Hyman Levy, p. 16, Hillway Publishing Company.
13. Ibid., p. 17.
14. *The Jewish Problem in the Soviet Union*, B. Z. Goldberg, pp. 356–57, Crown, 1961.
15. Ibid., pp. 357–58.
16. *The Jews in the Soviet Union*, Solomon Schwarz, p. 94, Syracuse University Press, 1951.
17. Ibid., p. 99.
18. *Jewish Workers and Farmers in the Crimea and Ukraine*, Evelyn Morrissey, pp. 22–23, JDC Publication, 1937.
19. *The Jews in the Soviet Union*, Solomon Schwarz, p. 174, Syracuse University Press, 1951.
20. *Conversations with Stalin*, Milovan Djilas, p. 187, Harcourt, Brace & World, 1962.
21. *The Kremlin, the Jews and the Middle East*, Judd L. Teller, p. 62, Thomas Yoseloff, 1957.
22. Ibid., p. 63.
23. Ibid., pp. 68, 70–72, 73, 74.
24. Ibid., p. 78.
25. *The Rise and Fall of Stalin*, Robert Payne, p. 740, Simon & Schuster (Avon), 1965.
26. London *Jewish Chronicle*, January 16, 1953.
27. *Moscow Journal*, Harrison Salisbury, University of Chicago Press.

28. New York *Times*, June 8, 1957.
29. *Conversations with Stalin*, Milovan Djilas, p. 188, Harcourt, Brace, & World, 1962.

CHAPTER IV

1. *Russia*, Harrison Salisbury, New York Times Byline Book, p. 92, Atheneum, 1965.
2. Oktiabr, *Minsk Daily*, February 1, 1929.
3. "The Jews, Problems of Communism," Zvi Gitelman, p. 92, September/October 1967. U. S. Information Agency.
4. Oktiabr, *Minsk Daily*, February 1, 1929.
5. "The Jews, Problems of Communism," Zvi Gitelman, p. 92, September/October 1967. U. S. Information Agency.
6. *Jews in Eastern Europe*, p. 10, July 1964.
7. B'nai B'rith news release, January 24, 1963.
8. Karl Yosifovich Yampolsky, *The Origin & Glass Essence of Jewish Rituals & Holidays* (tr. fr. Ukrainian), Society for the Diffusion of Political and Scientific Knowledge of the Ukrainian Soviet Socialist Republic, Kiev, 1962, p. 13–14.
9. *Znamia Kommunizma* (Odessa), September 10, 1959 (tr. fr. Russian).
10. Karl Yosifovich Yampolsky, *The Origin & Glass Essence of Jewish Rituals & Holidays*, (tr. fr. Ukrainian), Society for the Diffusion of Political and Scientific Knowledge of the Ukrainian Soviet Socialist Republic, Kiev, 1962, p. 23.
11. *Bugskaia Zaria*, October 13, 1959 (tr. fr. Russian).
12. *Znamia Kommunizma* (Odessa), September 10, 1959 (tr. fr. Russian).
13. *Lvovskaya Pravda*, December 14, 1958 (tr. fr. Russian).
14. *Jews in Eastern Europe*, July 1964, p. 27.
15. New York *Times*, October 26, 1967.
16. Item 1081, p. 162, Vol. VI, No. 20, *Religion in Communist Dominated Areas*, October 31, 1967, New York, N.Y.
17. Televised Press Conference, WNDT-TV Channel 13, April 26, 1967, New York, N.Y.
18. London *Jewish Chronicle*, November 22, 1963.

CHAPTER V

1. London *Jewish Chronicle*, November 3, 1967.
2. *Jews in the Soviet Union*, Solomon Rabinovich, Novosti Press Agency Publishing House, p. 45.
3. *The Legal Position of the Jewish Community of the Soviet Union*, Dr. William Korey, p. 6, B'nai B'rith.
4. New York *Herald Tribune*, November 18, 1963.
5. Jewish Congress Bi-Weekly, December 5, 1966.
6. London *Jewish Chronicle Literary Supplement*, December 8, 1967.
7. *The Legal Position of the Jewish Community of the Soviet Union*, Dr. William Korey, p. 13, B'nai B'rith, from Jerusalem *Post*, February 3, 1961.
8. *Jewish Life*, March 1958.
9. *Naie Presse*, April 27, 1958.
10. *Yiddish Kultur*, February 1959.
11. *Jews in Eastern Europe*, May 1965.
12. *Yiddish Kultur*, February 1959.
13. *Itogi vs esoyuznoi Perepisi Naseleniya 1959 goda* (1959 Census Results), published in Moscow, 1962, p. 184, table 53.
14. *Pechat v U.S.S.R.*, 1966.
15. United Press International, May 22, 1966.
16. Jewish Congress Bi-Weekly, December 5, 1966.
17. New York *Times*, September 12, 1967.
18. *The Legal Position of the Jewish Community in the Soviet Union*, Dr. William Korey, B'nai B'rith, p. 10, from *Pravda*, November 2, 1961.
19. New York *Times*, September 29, 1959.
20. *The Status of Jews in Soviet Education* by Dr. Nicholas De Witt, published by the Commission on International Affairs, American Jewish Congress.
21. *Midstream*, June/July 1967.
22. WNDT-TV, April 1967.
23. London *Jewish Chronicle*, June 24, 1966.

CHAPTER VI

1. *Jews in Eastern Europe*, May 1963.
2. *Midstream*, March 1965.

3. Journal of the International Commission of Jurists, Vol. V,
   #1, pp. 45–46, 1964.
4. *Sovietskaya Kirghizia,* January 9, 1962.
5. Ibid., June 25, 1962.
6. Journal of the International Commission of Jurists, Vol. I,
   p. 34.
7. *Jews in Eastern Europe,* May 1963.
8. *Izvestia,* October 20, 1963.
9. New York *Times,* February 27, 1964.

CHAPTER VII

1. *Newsweek,* August 21, 1967.
2. Brumberg, NCRAC Plenary Proceedings, June 29–July 21,
   1967.
3. Ibid., p. 5.
4. *The Jews in the Soviet Union,* Solomon Schwarz, Syracuse
   University Press, 1951, p. 117.
5. *Christian Science Monitor,* December 1967.
6. *Countdown in the Holy Land,* Lester Velie, Funk & Wagnalls,
   1969, p. 19.
7. Ibid., pp. 30–31.
8. London *Jewish Chronicle,* February 20, 1953.
9. *Sovietskaya Moldavia,* April 4, 1965.

CHAPTER X

1. Public Information Series, Department of State 3/10C, 367BT.
2. *Jews in Eastern Europe,* May 1967, p. 98.
3. Soviet Embassy Bulletin, Paris, December 5, 1966.
4. *Jews in Eastern Europe,* May 1967, p. 18.

SUGGESTED READING

BOOKS

Jews of Silence – Elie Wiesel – Holt, Rinehart & Winston
Between Hammer and Sickle – Arie L. Eliav – Signet
The Unredeemed – Ronald Rubin – Quadrangle
The Jews in the Soviet Union – Solomon Schwarz – Syracuse University Press
Confess, Confess – Yehoshua A. Gilboa – Little, Brown
The Jewish Problem in the Soviet Union – B. Z. Goldberg – Crown
House Without a Roof – Maurice Hindus – Doubleday
Ethnic Minorities in the Soviet Union – Frederick A. Praeger
    (Chapter – "Legal Position of Jewish Community in the Soviet
    Union," Dr. William Korey)

PERIODICAL

Jews in Eastern Europe, quarterly, 31 Percy St., London, W. 1

PAMPHLETS AND ARTICLES

White Paper – American Conference of Soviet Jewry, 55 West
    Forty-second St., New York City
Anti-Semitism in Eastern Europe – A Socialist International Publication 88a St. John's Wood High St., London
Israel and the Jews in the Soviet Mirror – Moshe Decter, Conference on the Status of Soviet Jews, 16 East Eighty-fifth St.,
    New York City
Anti-Semitism—Tool of Soviet Policy – Yaakov Moriah, The Organizations of Partisans, War Veterans and Nazi Victims, P. O.
    Box 3179, Tel Aviv, Israel

Ideology and History of Soviet Jewish Policy – Judd L. Teller, Farband, Labor Zionist Order, 575 Sixth Ave., New York City

The Council of Europe on the Jews in the Soviet Union – World Jewish Congress, London

Implications for Soviet Jewry in the Middle-East Crisis – National Community Relations Advisory Council, 55 West Forty-second St., New York Cty

Nationalities and Nationalism in the U.S.S.R.: The Jews – Zvi Gitelman Research Institute on Communist Affairs, School of International Affairs – Columbia University

ORGANIZATIONS

American Conference on Soviet Jewry, 55 West Forty-second St., New York City

Student Struggle for Soviet Jewry, 200 West Seventy-second St., New York City